Teetering on the Brink of Madness

Learning to Hear God

JEFF DAUGHERTY

ISBN 979-8-88540-105-0 (paperback)
ISBN 979-8-88540-106-7 (digital)

Christian Faith Publishing
832 Park Avenue
Meadville, PA 16335
www.christianfaithpublishing.com

Printed in the United States of America

This is my command—be strong and courageous! Do not be afraid or discouraged. For the Lord your God is with you wherever you go.

—Joshua 1:9

Contents

Introduction

Since the dawn of time, mankind has been trying to understand God.

What does he want from us?

What is the meaning of it all?

What must I do to please him?

Once I figure out how to please him, how do I stay in his good graces?

That is the tricky part now, isn't it?

There are 1,189 chapters in the Bible. We made it to chapter 3 before we blew it.

And don't blame it all on Eve. Adam was right next to her the whole time. Did he remind her of God's command?

Nope.

Did he tell her not to listen to the serpent?

Nope.

I can picture the scene now. After the serpent urges Eve to eat the fruit, she looks over at Adam and holds out the fruit to him. Adam shrugs and says, "What's the worst that could happen? You go first." So Eve takes a bite, and the rest is history.

There are 31,103 verses in the Bible, and we made it all the way to verse 62. That was the fall of man. It wasn't the moment when woman fell and was cursed with painful childbirth and short life while man roamed the garden for all time in his nakedness. They lived together, and they fell together. Adam is just as guilty as Eve.

That sounds pretty awful, doesn't it? We only made it to verse 62. Try throwing this into the mix. God did not create man until verse 27, so Adam and Eve only needed 35 verses to cause the fall of mankind.

And here you sit, thinking that you alone are faced with the uncertainty of knowing what God wants from us. What makes you so different from the 110 billion people that have walked the earth since that moment when Eve ate the fruit from the tree of knowledge?

Do you still think you are alone?

You are not alone.

People have been searching for God for most of our recorded history. Some just want to please God. Some are just curious. Some want answers to life's most difficult questions. And of course, there are some who have claimed to speak to God in an effort to gain control over others. Great rulers have often told their people that they alone can hear what God has to say. They say that all people must bow to their rule if they want to stay in God's good graces.

Adam could hear from God, and look how that turned out. Some people take this to mean that if you are blessed enough to hear from God, you had better not mess it up. Being a Christian does not mean you have to be perfect, and it most certainly does not mean you have to treat others as though you are perfect.

There was only one man that was ever perfect. He was not crucified for his actions. He was not forced to die as a lesson to others. He went willingly. He was perfect. He paid the price for our sins. He died for us.

Do you question your worth? Do you wonder if you are worthy of such a gift? Consider this. Christ was not sacrificed for all of us. He was sacrificed for *each* of us. Each one of us was judged as worthy of the sacrifice that he made. That is how he views your worth.

You are a precious child of God even if you are not yet a believer. He knows our hearts. He knows what keeps us away from him, but it is not how worthy *he* finds *us* that causes us problems. It is how worthy we find ourselves.

The simple truth is that God loves you. You are worthy of the sacrifice of Jesus Christ. He knows this. We hesitate because we do not see that same worth in ourselves. That is the first obstacle we must overcome. We must get past our own self-worth.

I know what you are thinking: *It is not that simple* or maybe *But you don't know what I've done in my past.* No, I don't—but God does.

Do you think that when God wants to see you, you can shout, "Just a minute," while you sweep all your skeletons into your closet? Do you really believe that you can hide from God? He is not going to barge in on you to catch you in the act. He is waiting for you to accept him.

You are loved. God is waiting for you to take him by the hand and follow wherever he may lead. He is extending his hand to you. You only have to take it.

Your prayers are heard.

Your prayers are answered.

Think of it this way: Do you remember your earliest memory? Do you remember your parents looking after you and preparing you for what lies ahead in life? Do you remember how they did their best to provide for your every need? That was their job, right? That is what a parent is supposed to do. They give you the education that you need so you can stand on your own. Whatever you needed, they provided.

God the Father is not that different. Whatever your purpose in life, he will ensure that you have what you need to succeed. What does that mean? He will make sure we have what we need if we put our faith and trust in him.

"God, please help me find a job. I just got laid off and desperately need the work."

Prayer answered. Manual labor—oh, goody.

"God, it's me again. Can you please help me find a different job? I don't like this one."

Prayer answered—even if it may take a while.

"God, please help me to get a car so I can get back and forth to work. It takes too long to take the bus, and walking is too hard."

Prayer answered in the form of a car from the late eighties—big rust spots, with rattles and squeaks coming from every nook and cranny.

"God, I hate to bother you again, but can you help me to get a nicer car? Please?"

Before long, we have a better job and a nicer car, and we wonder why we never hear from God and why our prayers aren't being answered.

He will make sure that we have food to eat and shelter over our heads. That does not mean that he will put us up in a really nice condo at the beach. It may be that he will open a friend's door to you when you need it the most. How about that few hours of overtime that provides just enough extra money to buy some groceries? Whatever we need, he provides—even if it is a beat-up car from the eighties. It may not be necessarily what we want, but it will be what we need.

We have our own expectations that tend to get in the way. God is not Santa Claus. We don't give him a list of things we want and complain if we don't get what we ask for. These are not demands for God; they are prayers. Just ask him with an open and honest heart. He answers our prayers even if the answer is sometimes no.

The problem is that most people need to learn to hear what God is telling them. God often speaks to us. The problem is that we do not realize it. Have you ever had an idea pop into your head and you just wonder, "Where did that come from?" Of course, not all of these are from God. When you first start listening to God, that is the way it feels. As you learn, you can begin to tell the difference between what you are thinking and what God is telling you.

We need to differentiate between what we want and what God wants. We have our ideas and plans for our life. Be careful not to turn your plans into God's plans. God has his own plans for us. He does not ask us our opinions. The people that we think are the best choices really are. They are the best choice for the purpose that God has for them. He will teach us what we need to know in order to serve his purpose.

But you have questions, right? There are some things that you do not understand. Don't make the mistake of making demands of God. It is called faith for a reason. Just trust that he will give you the answers that you need when you need them. I know that when my time on earth is done, I will have many questions. I just accept that there are some things that I just don't have all of the answers for.

When God wants you to know something, He will tell you. Believe me. He will teach you whatever he wants you to learn.

But why should you trust me?

I studied business in college, not theology. I studied more business in grad school, but still no theology.

I went to a Christian university. Does that count? Maybe I learned about this by osmosis—just by being close to Christian professors with great knowledge.

I wanted to open a bakery. This was not on my list of what I wanted to be when I grew up. This is not the line I got in at the career fair. A little bakery and coffee shop—I would have been quite content with that. My passion has been baking. I have no desire to open a donut shop. I wanted to open something a little different—cinnamon rolls, scones, cheesecakes. That would have been a pretty good gig. Of course, my MBA didn't cover cookies. I prayed that God would show me my path. Business didn't seem to be going very far. I figured that if I was going to struggle, I would enjoy what I was doing. Other than having a workday that started at 4:00 a.m., it sounded like a great plan.

But it was my plan, not God's plan. If anything, history should have taught me that my plans seldom work out. You see, I did not start out by being a regular church attendee who gained great knowledge as I grew with the church and with God. You expect to hear that from some people. They are the people that you see as deacons or church leaders of some sort. They are the ones that you think would be ideal candidates.

For me, it was continued prayer. Keep in mind prayer sometimes comes out as screaming in frustration or despair for God to help us. Many of my prayers came out that way. I did not see them as prayers at the time, but God still heard my cries. Even if we do not realize it, he hears it when we cry out to him.

The answer to our prayers may often be no, but sometimes it is yes, and yes is not what we expect it to be.

I found God. I learned to hear him speak to me. Did you catch that? I *learned.* It was not a wave of a magic wand and *poof*—I could hear God. I had to learn. He had to teach me.

It was not a journey through tulips and bunny rabbits.

It was difficult.

There were highs and lows.

Everyone's journey is different. For some, it is as sudden as a light bulb going off. For others, it is a long and difficult road with many twists and turns; and for others still, it is like a lifelong education that continues to build.

For me, it was much different. I had never heard of another journey quite like mine. What God had to teach me, I was not prepared for.

It was the single most difficult journey of my life. God wanted me to trust him. My belief in God had always been accompanied by clauses that I had added as if it were a contract. I was a reluctant believer. I was willing to believe in God, but there were certain things I was not ready to give in to, some things I was not ready to let go of.

When I was fresh out of high school, I joined the Marine Corps. The method of training for the Marines was to break everyone down to their lowest form. They stripped away personal identity and backgrounds. Gone were the different classes of society.

I hate to bring up math, but the first step in working with fractions is to find the lowest common denominator. That is the way the Marine Corps begins their training. They break all the new recruits down until they are all equal in their most basic form. They do it because it works.

In my journey to find God, I had conditions and demands. I had even been so bold as to tell God, "If you are real, prove it!"

God was very patient with me. He waited until I was ready to believe—not because he had met my demands but because I had reached my lowest and most vulnerable state.

I was so broken that I had been ready to believe no matter what the cost. I only asked him to help me. I would do anything he asked of me. It was my surrender to God.

Before God would allow me to walk along the path that he had set for me, I had to step out of the boat into the midst of the most frightening storm I had ever witnessed. It was a storm that drove me right up to the brink of madness.

His plan for me started well before I ever thought possible. You see, God gave me the title for this book almost twenty-five years ago. I knew the title before I had any desire to write a book, before I really knew what that madness entailed. I wandered close enough to the precipice of madness that I was seriously contemplating getting a psychiatrist.

I chose to see my pastor instead.

PART 1

Living in Darkness

I barely hear their voices anymore. I hardly ever hear their call to me in the blackness of the night. I sleep in relative peace for the first time in many years. They are still there. I hear their voices still but have to pay close attention to recognize the voices. Such quiet voices are very easy for me to ignore. I have many tricks up my sleeve that allow the voices to fade into an unintelligible murmur.

I have begged and prayed for years to hear the nothingness that I now have. I am well protected and insulated against the darkness that has tormented me for so long.

But still I struggle.

Without saying a word more, there are a few of you who know exactly what I speak of. They are a very few, to be sure. There are a few more who do not know exactly what I speak of, but you understand the feeling behind it.

Most of you have no idea of what I speak.

Do I speak of voices as a metaphor for life's struggles?

Not this time.

Or maybe the voices I speak of are of my own creation. Maybe they are the voices we hear when we talk to ourselves. We all do it from time to time. Anytime we have a decision to make, we talk to ourselves as if in a council meeting where we debate the right course of action.

That is certainly a reasonable guess.

Reasonable—but still incorrect.

Newfound Purpose

All my life I have waited to discover my purpose in this world. I know we all have our place. We all have a purpose that is set before us. Discovering that purpose can be a maddening endeavor all by itself. So many people make it all the way through their lives, never having discovered what that purpose is—or more accurately, they have failed to realize what that purpose is.

Our path may not have the magnificent splendor of a great movie or play the way we often think it should. It may be a quiet and humble path with very little recognition or appreciation. Our path may be to provide the support and love for someone who desperately needs it. Each piece is a part of a greater puzzle. It is a puzzle that is often beyond our ability to see any piece but the one we hold. It is a small piece, but it is critical to the overall picture.

Think of an Olympic torch being run across the country before lighting the flame at the opening ceremonies. We all want our purpose to be glorious like the person who runs up the steps to light the flame. You never think of the countless people who carried the torch along the way.

We are the torch bearers for the light of Christ. I will carry this flame held high before me as the light of Christ deserves. I carry this flame not because I am asked to carry it. I carry this light because it is the same light that called me out of the darkness. It is the same light that gave me a chance at a new life.

At first I saw the light as some mirage that I was unsure was real, but once I felt the warm glow of the light upon my face, I clung to it like a life preserver, keeping my head above the waves for the first time in a stormy sea that surrounded me.

That light saw me through the darkness. It carried me above the waves. It lit up a world that I never knew existed.

And now that I know what that word is, I want to share it with the world. I want to shout it from the mountaintops.

I want everyone who has ever felt the darkness closing in around them to see the light as I have seen it.

I will carry this torch along whatever path the Lord directs me, for it is his light that I carry, and it is my hope that others will see it as I have. It is not my light I share. It is as if I have lit a candle in my window, so anyone who passes by may see it and has a renewal of hope—a glimmer of light in the midst of their darkness.

It is in that darkness that our story begins. It is the darkness that surrounded me for most of my life. It is the same darkness that surrounds many of you.

If we can understand the darkness, we can begin to.

Reaching for His Robe

Several years ago, I was in a very difficult place in my life. I was unemployed. I had few prospects. I felt alone. I had family, but that was not what I really needed. I had seen other people with such deep faith that carried them through trying times like these. I grew up in a Christian household, going to church every Sunday and being a part of a youth group. When I became an adult, that all changed. I believed in God, but I didn't know God. I had never heard from him. I began to question everything I knew.

Life is full of questions. Some are easy and quickly answered. They pass us a thousand times a day.

"Do I take the door on the left or the one on the right?"

Some are hard but can still be answered.

"Why is the sky blue?"

A difficult question to be sure—but it has an answer. Not everyone knows what that answer is. Others will be more than happy to share the answer with you, and some simply don't care. They just accept that it is, and they move on to other things.

Some questions are downright complicated. They can be debated to no end and often are. These are the questions that people have been asking since the dawn of time. These are the questions of life and existence, how we came to be and what our purpose is. These are topics that can be discussed in great detail. They affect all of humanity.

But what about me? What is my purpose? This is much more personal and often very private. It is not discussed at parties or family gatherings. We don't discuss it at the office. Wherever we began in life or whatever our upbringing, there comes a point in our lives that we kneel on the floor and look to the heavens with desperate wonder.

"Why am I here?"

"Why is life so hard?"

"What is the point of it all?"

We all need something to believe in. I grew up in a Christian family, going to church on Sundays and again on Wednesdays. Growing up in a family like this, you are taught from an early age many explanations and answers to these questions.

But there comes a time in a persons' life that they have to decide for themselves what to believe in. Many turn away from their Christian upbringing when they make these decisions. I did.

I tried everything I could think of. I researched other religions. Would one of them hold the answers that I seek? How about leaving organized religions in favor of becoming a spiritualist? Something has got to work, right? There has to be something out there that can make sense of this maddening depression. Still, I heard nothing—no answers, no helping hand, nothing.

Suicide is something that I could never do. It was not an option in any way. Still, I can understand how people end up in that place.

Where was God when I needed him most? To be clear, I believed in God; but deep down, I had no idea who he was and what he wanted from me. To be honest, I didn't even know for certain if he had any idea who I was. My life was spiraling down the tubes. I saw no God reaching in to help me. No matter how loud I screamed for help or how often, I heard nothing. No answers came to me. Moses had a burning bush. Joseph and Mary had an angel appear before them. But me? Not a whisper to be heard. Not a signal to be followed. Nothing but profound silence.

I begged.

I pleaded.

Eventually, I gave up. Doubt crept into my mind. If God were real, wouldn't he want me to know it instead of abandoning me? I consider myself an intelligent person. If you look hard enough, you will find some evidence to support what you want to believe in. You find things to justify your actions. Until I had proof that God was real, then I would assume he wasn't.

But when life gets unbearable, you need somewhere to turn, someone to blame. No matter how much I told myself otherwise, I believed in God. I also believed that he wanted nothing to do with me. So be it. "God, if you are really there and are listening to me… please don't let me wake up in the morning. I am tired. There is nothing here for me. Please let me go."

Have you ever been there in that dark place?

Deep down I believed in God. I continued to pray. My prayer became a routine part of my night. Every evening was the same. During this period, I was often unemployed. Those times were by far the worst. I would make sure my laptop and list of job search notes were ready. I would program the coffee pot for an early start. I would make my rounds of the house to ensure that all of the windows and doors were locked, and as I made my way slowly through the house, I would pray. It was a dark, sad, and lonely prayer. It was a prayer that God would show me mercy and end my misery.

I went on this way for quite a long time. I would pray to a God that I wasn't entirely certain was even there. I would work when I had a job. I did not see any of the beauty in the world. I saw none of the blessings that I still had. There was nothing but a slow trudge through the quicksand of my life.

I know some of you can relate exactly to what I am talking about. You know the darkness just as well as I do. You get to a point where the darkness becomes a comfort to you. You soon begin to fear any life outside the security of your dark little prison—and a prison is exactly what it is.

All I had was my own fragile faith that he was even real. It was that tiny sliver of faith that kept me going at all.

Sometime later, I found a job at a construction company. I also returned to school. Things slowly started to improve, but things for this small business were deteriorating. The owner of the company, a man of great faith, was in poor health. He had no one that he could rely upon to run things while he was out. The managers were all in conflict. I volunteered to take over as general manager.

Things were tough, but we did our best to keep things going. During this time, I met the woman who would become my wife. We planned our wedding. I was happy, but the economy turned south, and things got difficult. We had to cancel our wedding. We instead had a small ceremony at our church.

Eventually, we had to close the company, and I was left unemployed and scarred by failure. All of the anxiety that I had worked so hard to put behind me came boiling up to the surface, but this time, I was married. She had married me even though I was losing my job.

The most difficult part of closing the business was the people. I had the responsibility to tell the entire company that we were closing. Some of the employees had been with the company for more than thirty years. I realize now, all these years later, that there were several factors that contributed to the closing of the company; but at the time, I was plagued by feelings of failure. I felt as though I had let down all the people who had put their trust in me.

Everything I had tried had failed. My career was in chaos. I applied for work but was told I was overqualified or did not have enough experience. My confidence was shattered. I had let everyone down. I could not let my wife down too. I just couldn't.

One afternoon, while my wife, Kelly, was at work, I had hit bottom. I had no solutions. I had no ideas. The only confidence I had was in the fact that whatever I could try would probably fail. I had the television playing in the background and had somehow gotten on a show about Peter. It was during the time when he was imprisoned in Rome. He had been talking to his guards about Christ and forgiveness.

I collapsed in a heap on the floor. Completely broken, I cried out to the God I really didn't know.

I wanted him to be real. I needed him to be real.

I wanted something to be real.

Anything.

I surrendered.

It was total and absolute—mind, body, and spirit together in one final desperate act.

I surrendered my life and everything I was and would ever be. There I was kneeling on the floor of my living room. Tears were streaming down my face as I reached out *through* my pain and called to God. I pleaded with him. All I wanted was to know that he was real. I wanted to hear from him, and most of all, I wanted some purpose for my life. I would do anything he asked of me. I just wanted purpose and meaning. I wanted *his* purpose.

I asked him if he would still take me as his own.

That was the moment that everything had changed. My life would never be the same again.

I felt better—not completely but a little bit. When you are that low, a little seems like the world.

I pulled myself together as best I could.

For the next few weeks, that one plea rang through my mind: "I will do anything you ask. I just need to know that you are real and that you will help me."

It was not long after that, for the first time, I heard God speak to me. It was a thought that sprang from nowhere. It came immediately after another plea to God for mercy. I would do anything he asked—if only he would help me.

"Jeffrey, be careful what you ask for."

That was not what I expected.

Nightmares

I had spent my entire life looking for someone like Kelly. She has become my best friend. Many married couples tell you that they are best friends. There are those that will tell you that marriage is hard work, and for most, I would venture to guess that it is quite true. But for Kelly and I, it is different. For us, marriage is not hard work at all. It is the most comfortable and natural thing in the world. Genesis 2:24 says that when a man and woman are united as husband and wife, they become one flesh. Sometimes it feels like she really is my other half. There are times when we leave each other for work in the morning, and it is just a little difficult to breathe.

The thought of letting her down and failing her took me to the lowest I had ever gotten.

That was a turning point for me.

Rock bottom.

I had been living in a world of darkness for countless years, but this was the first time that someone else depended on me.

Before Kelly, I was in a depression that was so deep that I felt as if there was nobody else in the world but me. Kelly made the world brand-new. It gave me hope for a future that I had not really known before.

The darkness I dwelled in before Kelly was all I had really known. My days were spent in depression. My nights were filled with nightmares.

Not just any nightmares—they were so terrifying that I thought they would drive me insane.

They started long before that moment on my living room floor, before the depression, before things in my life began spinning out of control. They haunted my dreams. They became so frequent that I became numb to the fear and horror. They were the beginning of my descent into the fringes of madness.

Nighttime has always been a turbulent time for me. I am not sure when it began or why. There is no specific event in my past that led to my nightly torment. I am not afraid of the dark. There is and no logical explanation for it. I have always had trouble falling asleep. I have never really had any problems with staying asleep, but falling asleep could easily take an hour or more. My mind was always racing from place to place and topic to topic. I would start thinking about what I had to do the next day. This is common for most people. I think we all get caught up in the potential hurdles we would have to face the next day, but that is not the only place my mind would wander. I would think of crazy stories and animals that Dr. Seuss would be proud of.

Think of it like a shopping spree. You have $500 to spend in the mall, and you have an hour to spend everything, or you lose it. You would begin with a quick stroll through the mall, hitting all of your favorite stores. After a brief stop at those, you begin moving on to the others. As the hour slips by, you think of a few things you may have missed at stores you have already been to. Your quick stroll soon turns into a slight jog. The minutes tick by one by one. Faster and faster they seem to go. As the time slips by, you begin to lose focus of what you were looking for as you try to sort through the jumbled shopping list in your mind. With time nearly up, you are running at a sprint for stores that were not even on your list. Your mind ends up whirling in circles. You are exhausted from the run. You think of the items that you are carrying with you. You suddenly think of something at the other end of the mall that you want. So now you are going through all the items you carry and decide to leave some of the items so you can move more quickly to your new target. You are now sprinting for all you are worth, but by now, that sprint is a fair bit slower than your quick stroll. It feels like a sprint because you are putting all of your effort into keeping up the pace, but it continues to slow until you just can't move anymore.

That is what my mind does when it is time for me to go to sleep. It is constantly racing and whirling past so many things that it is difficult to focus on just one. It continues until I am so exhausted that I finally drift off to sleep. For many years, I have tried to harness this sixty minutes of chaos as if I could close it up in a box. The only way I have been able to do this is by focusing on something else. Sometimes it is an elaborate fictitious tale that continues night after night. It was all I could do to keep my mind from racing.

I cannot be certain why I have had such a difficult time getting to sleep. I am not a psychologist. I am not a psychiatrist, and I may be wrong, but the nightmares might explain a thing or two.

I am honestly not sure when the nightmares began. I have had them for at least the past twenty-five years. There was no traumatic experience, to my knowledge, that gave the dreams their start. An argument could be made that they are the result of watching violent movies. Perhaps violent video games could be the culprit. To be sure, they are both filled with acts of incomprehensible horror.

But then again, so is the nightly news.

Do you dream in color?

Can you smell things like flowers or fresh-baked bread in your dreams?

Can you feel things in your dreams? If you kicked a coffee table in your dream, would it hurt? For me, the answer to all of these questions is yes. My dreams are a place of vivid reality. The sounds and smells fill the senses.

Other things feel quite real in my dreams—things like pain and fear.

I now trust God completely. I know he has a purpose for the things he does. I know he has a plan for my life. If there is something that he wants me to know, he will teach me. But looking back on the nightmares, I wonder. What was I supposed to learn from those nightmares? Was that even God's doing? Was the enemy trying to drive me insane, or was it all in my head? Was there something in my life that had caused these horrible dreams?

In some of my dreams, there is a common feature like a building or street. I have had many dreams that use the same building but in different settings or sizes. They are always completely unique themes. There are no commonalities at all with the exception of the building. One would think there is something significant about this. I, for one, have no idea.

I will try to be as detailed and accurate as possible; however, some of these dreams have occurred many years ago, and my memory and notes are only so good. With that being said, everything I am writing is completely true.

So, without further ado, let me lie back on the couch and tell you about a few of these nightmares. You can grab a seat and put your best detective hat on and figure out what it all means.

Dream number 1

In this dream, I heard a loud crash coming from outside. I got out of bed and slowly walked to the window of my bedroom. There was no light shining from the street lights. As I peeked out through the curtains, I noticed that there were no lights coming from the other houses. It was completely dark with the exception of the faint glow from the moon. As if I was alarmed by the lack of lights in the neighborhood, I spun around quickly to take an inventory of all the electronic devices in my room.

The room was small and square with the head of my bed against the wall with the bedroom door on the wall to the left with the window on the wall to the right. On the opposite wall from the bed, just in the door to the left, was my dresser with an alarm clock on the left side. The alarm clock was blank.

On the wall just to the right of the window was a small bookcase with two shelves. There was a small stereo sitting on the top. The little light on the stereo was not its usual red. To the left of the shelf, I could see the power cord stretching to an outlet beneath the window.

I had to gather my nerve to walk toward my bedroom door. My hand reached out for the knob, and as it began to turn, I heard a loud crash coming from the living room at the far end of the house. I darted back toward the window and could tell from the commotion that the noise was from someone or something crashing through the front door of my house. I took a quick step toward my bed and slid to the floor with a roll that put me underneath and looking toward the bottom of my bedroom door.

From my hiding spot under the bed, I could hear some of the noise from the living room and more from the window. It was a lot like listening to a stereo, but while listening, the balance shifts from one speaker to the other. In this case, I could hear the noise becoming louder in the living room and quieter from the window. I stared at the bedroom door with quick glances to the window.

I could hear things being thrown around and broken at the other end of the house. All at once, I rolled out from under the bed and flew toward the window. I do not remember unlocking the window. All I remember is climbing through and running from the front of the house.

Parked along the street in front of the house next door was a bus. It was the house immediately to the left as I faced the street (just in case you are keeping track). It looked like a commuter bus. It had huge windows along the sides, and the back window was equally as huge—almost as if it was meant to give the riders a good view of the surrounding area like they were on a sight-seeing tour. I have no idea what it was doing in my neighborhood in the middle of the night. Come to think of it, the neighborhood itself was completely unfamiliar to me. Not that it matters when some big scary monster or beast is thrashing my house.

The next thing I know, I am on the bus, ducking as low as possible so as to not be seen in the giant windows. I was hiding between the seats in one of the back rows of the bus. I could hear the beast smash through what was left of the front door. My breathing was rapid, and my heart beat so loudly that I thought it would give away my hiding spot. Somehow, I knew that the beast was looking for me. Just as strange, the noises were so loud that the entire neighborhood should be outside, trying to identify the source. But there was no one there. The growling (for lack of a better way to describe it) got louder as the beast approached the bus.

The fear was overwhelming at this point, and the last thing I remember was the bus rocking as the beast smashed into it. That was the moment I woke up. My breathing was heavy. My heart raced, and I was sweating like I had been physically running the beast. My mind raced as I looked for a notepad to document what I had seen in my dream. It took me nearly half an hour to describe the ordeal. Ever since that night, I have kept the journal in my nightstand next to the bed.

I am sorry to give you such a story only to leave you without an ending. Such is the way of nightmares. This was not the first nor was it the last. There were many dreams like this one—always with me being chased by some big unseen monster.

Dream number 2

This dream was the scariest one I have ever had. In fact, it cannot even be called a dream. It was a nightmare, pure and simple. The fundamental difference between this nightmare and others is the fact that there is someone else at the mercy of evil besides me.

I am not sure who she was, the girl in the nightmare. I never saw her face. I could tell that I knew her, but beyond that, I do not know how. It is one thing to be chased by monsters in your dreams. It is another, entirely, to have someone else being tortured while you are forced to sit next to them.

Yes, you heard me correctly. She was being tortured. The first scene in this horrible tale begins with me sitting in the front passenger seat of a large SUV. My arms and hands are twisted and tied to the back seat. However I was tied into the seat, it was effective. I could not move a muscle. I was gagged so I couldn't speak. I was facing forward, unable to turn around and unable to see, but I could hear everything—every horrible scream. I was nighttime, probably in the wee hours of the morning. We were in a parking lot. The lot was mostly empty. For all the cars that were in the lot, there were no people.

The monster, in this case, was a man. At least he looked like a man. He was in the driver's seat as we pulled into the parking lot. We were in the back of the lot. There was a small road running around the lot and the building. There was a small median of grass separating the lot and the road. The lot was dimly lit with trees spaced about twenty yards apart on the median. There were a few trash cans spaced along the median at about every third tree or so. There were very few lights on the road or building so everything was dimly lit.

The driver taunted me by telling me everything he was going to do to the young woman. He had a knife in his hands and would press the blade near my face and throat as he spoke. Apparently, she could hear everything he said because her screams grew louder. Eventually, he tired of taunting me and moved to the back of the truck. The seats were folded forward, and she was lying down in the back with her hands and feet tied.

I am not sure what exactly he did to her. All I know for sure is that her screams were haunting. They were filled with pain and fear, to be sure, but also with a sense of hopelessness. It was that kind of hopelessness that says staying alive is no longer your focus. You just want it to stop.

The next thing I knew, we were both inside the building, each of us strapped to a table, knife wounds all over us. Blood was everywhere. She was no longer screaming. It would seem that her pain finally ended. I could not see the driver. I struggled to move my hands, trying to break free.

After what seemed like hours, I managed to break my hand lose. I did not see what happened next. I do not know if I checked the girl. I do not know if the driver was still there. All I remember was running from the building. I stopped near one of the trashcans beside a tree and through some bloodied rags that were hanging from my wrists. The truck was still there. The driver was nowhere to be seen—almost like he had done what he came for and simply vanished. I looked through the truck for keys or a phone—anything I could use to call for help. I found a phone on the floor of the truck and opened it to call the police.

That was when I woke up. I do not know what this nightmare means. I do not know what caused it. Having someone else at risk made the whole thing much worse than it would have been if I had been alone.

These dreams continued for some time. I would have them to varying degrees of scariness, about two or three times a week. The more nightmares I had, the less fearful I became of them. They just were. I would have a horrible nightmare that, once upon a time, would have kept me from going back to sleep for days. But I would just wake up with a small jump and sit up in bed and say, "Wow, that one was pretty weird." Then I would lie back down and go back to sleep.

Dream number 3

This dream felt different. I am not sure exactly why. Okay, that is not entirely true. I know exactly why it felt different, but there is more to it than that. Allow me to explain.

As usual, I am being chased by something. In the past, it felt like a monster or big evil force. This time was a bit different. For starters, I am with a group of people. There are five of us in all—three men and two women. All three of the men seamed fairly clean cut and of average height and build. One had a dirty-blond, bordering on light-brown, hair. The other had dark-brown hair that was almost black, and I had brown hair. The two women were slender and between five feet two inches and five feet seven inches. One had blonde hair and the other brown.

All five of us appeared to be in our late twenties to midthirties. We were all wearing comfortable clothes that were suitable for a day of hiking or hanging out among friends at a barbeque. Our clothes were fairly clean, like we had been wearing them a day or two at the most. We appeared to be friends that had known each other for a long time. None of the friends looked familiar to me.

We looked to be in the ruins of a good-sized city—not a New York or Chicago-sized place by any means. Most buildings were between three and six stories tall. There were no trees or grass in sight. All of the buildings looked to be in ruins. The block was crumbling and the windows long since shattered and missing. There were a few doors going into the buildings, but most were either gone completely or just barely hanging by one remaining hinge. The few doors that looked to be intact had no locks or handles of any kind. The entire area was devoid of people, animals, or anything of value.

We were five friends, alone and being hunted. We were running through the streets like we were trying to stay ahead of something, but there was no sign of anything behind us. We simply ran from building to building and hiding place to hiding place, trying not to get caught. The light of the day was beginning to fade along with our energy.

We were running down a street that was about four lanes across. It looked like a typical downtown street in any American City. We came to an intersection with a narrow side street and came to a stop, all of us looking around us with several glances behind us. We were leaning against the building next to us or slightly bent over with our hands on our knees, trying to catch our breath. "Come on, we need to get off the street," someone said.

The narrow street had buildings on both sides that were between four and eight stories. The street was wide enough to park cars along both curbs and leave enough room for a single vehicle to pass. It was the type of road where you would have to pull over to let an oncoming vehicle pass. But like the rest of the city, the whole street was deserted. About a half block down the narrow street, there was a building on the right side with a door still hanging. It was a larger building with a few openings leading to the inside. The door that we found opened to a small room. It looked like it could have been a storage room at one point. It was about the size of a small bedroom. There were no other doors or windows leading out of the room.

We looked around to make sure we weren't seen although looking back on it, I am not sure what we were looking back for. We never saw anyone or anything behind us. But still, in the dream, we always knew something was right behind us.

We entered the room with the last person closing the door behind them. The door fit tightly and with a shove was fairly secure. At least it was secure enough that the wind would not blow the door open. The five of us sat down, leaning against the walls. We just sat there for what seemed like hours, staring at the walls, each of us alone in our own thoughts. Maybe we were all daydreaming of a better time long since passed. One of the women had a small backpack at her side.

Just then, the man with the dirty-blond hair spoke up, "We have to do it again. It's time."

"No! I can't do it anymore," the woman with the pack said.

"We have to. It is the only chance we have left. They are too close. We can't afford to get caught."

"We have no choice," the other woman said.

The remaining two of the group just listened in silence. We all knew what had to be done, but all of us, even the man with the dirty-blond hair, was terrified of the thought.

"I don't want to do it any more than you do," he said. "But the only chance we have is to reset and start over. That is the only way we can stay ahead of them."

"I know," she said. "I just want it to be over. I'm tired and I'm scared and I hate that thing."

We were all just shaking our heads in agreement as the woman placed the pack in the center of the group. "Me too," one of the men said as he reached for the pack.

Out of the pack, he pulled a small black revolver. His hand was shaking horribly. "I don't know if I can do it, but we have to. It is the only way."

He closed his eyes tight. Tears were running down his face as he lifted the revolver to his temple.

The loud crack of the revolver was deafening in the small room. One by one, they lifted the revolver to their heads, some to their temples and some to their foreheads. When it was my turn, I reached for the revolver that was lying next to the person to my right. I held it up to my forehead and slowly squeezed the trigger. That one terrifying moment seemed to last an eternity.

What was most unusual about the whole ordeal was the shot itself. I could feel everything as if it was in slow motion. I could feel the pressure of the bullet against my forehead. Slowly the pressure became heat. The heat grew more and more intense. After becoming quite hot, the heat slowly moved from the surface of my forehead along a path to the back of my head. It moved until my whole head was burning with a fire that had no flames.

The heat was what made me wake up. I had been growing pretty numb to the fear of nightmares, but this was completely different. In all of the dreams I had been having over the years, I had never been caught by anything. To be honest, I hadn't exactly been caught by anything this time either.

I had no idea what this was supposed to mean. I have had a few people say since then that it was an awakening of my mind. Although that is an explanation of sorts, I am not sure what that means either.

At that point in my life, I had not yet surrendered to God, so my thoughts did not go toward any godly purpose or direction. At times I wondered if this was what it was like to lose your mind.

With no ideas or solutions, I simply sat there, teetering on the brink of madness.

On the Brink

Proceed with caution all who enter here, for darkness and madness dwell in the places we are about to walk. Like a maze, this place is with twists and turns at every step and fear and torment around each and every corner. Find your way through the maze using help wherever you can find it, and you will escape its clutches. If you do not find the elusive source of help from within the maze, forever will you be trapped by the madness and torment.

Perhaps I am being a little overly dramatic.

First at the ready to assault your sanity is music, soft and mysterious, playing from some unknown source. No sounds of radios from my house or the next. No nearby cars or passersby—just music, soft and steady.

Then come voices calling out to you from the blackness. They are soft and nonthreatening like the tales of the sirens in legends of long ago.

Refuse them, and their soft and comforting words become an endless barrage of pain and torment. These words will be endless and without mercy. Your every flaw and weakness is at their disposal. Every skeleton in your past that you thought was so carefully hidden away and forgotten is now a weapon for them to use against you.

If you manage to get past the voices without falling into complete madness, a face to go with those voices soon appears—but it is not a face in the normal sense. It is a dark and evil shadow that spills into your room like a poisonous gas. It is a shadow so dark that in the pitch black of night, you still see them as if they are a blackness beyond any you have seen before.

Sounds exciting, yes?

Imagine you are walking down a long hallway. At the end of the hall, there are two doors—one on the left and another on the right. The door on the left leads to the office of a prominent psychiatrist. The door on the right leads to your local pastor's office. Which door do I choose?

Left door? Right door?

Whichever door I choose would set my path for the rest of my life.

I chose to rely on God for direction. I chose to meet with my pastor, Steve. But what would I have to talk to a pastor about? Dreams? Not this time. This time I was worried about the unraveling of my mind. I was about to go off the deep end. It was not dreams or things that happened in my mind that were causing such great anxiety. This time, the things that tormented me began to happen when I was awake—but we will get to that later.

For now, fast forward a few years. It has been about four years since the time of my nightmares. I am now happily married. We have just started going to church—my wife for the first time and I for the first time since I was a teenager. We are both new to how God works and why. Life is still pretty tumultuous.

When my wife and I were planning our wedding, I had to close my business. I found myself, once again, unemployed. We canceled our big wedding celebration and instead had a pastor at our church perform the ceremony with no one in attendance other than my parents. It was very small but nice. In marriage, I could not have been happier; but in life, things were much less stable.

I had viewed the closing of my business and my own personal failure. I used to work for a small company that began to go through financial difficulties when the owner began to have health problems. At first I took over as general manager so we could at least try to fix things. We made some improvements but were still struggling. I had just graduated with my MBA. I had the degree but not the experience. We did the best we could under such difficult circumstances. When the owner decided to close the company, I and two other long-time employees took over the business in an effort to save it. When we started, we had about a month of life left in us. We made it nearly three years. The three of us did everything we could. We used every resource we had. Credit cards were maxed. Savings were depleted.

Had we started three years earlier, we may have had a better chance. This was about the time that the economy started to crumble. We could turn around a struggling company, or we could weather the storm of a major recession—but we could not do both.

In the end, we closed the business. It was a painful experience. I took the whole thing very personally. I withdrew from everyone but my wife. She was all I had. She was all I truly wanted. She was all that made me happy. But I not only felt like I failed the employees of my business; I felt like I failed her too. We got married at a time when I didn't have a job.

That was when I crumbled and sank to my knees in surrender. It was my absolute surrender to God and his will. I would do anything he asked of me. I could no longer manage things myself. Everything I had tried had failed.

When I got out of the Marine Corps in 1995, I got into the computer field. That was when the technology bubble burst and computer companies began to close at an alarming rate. The company I worked for was sold to an out-of-state competitor. None of the employees were retained. After a short period of unemployment, I found a new job with a well-funded start-up. Things were looking promising—for a little while anyway.

After about a year, they decided that they were not making the money that they had hoped and decided to close. I found myself unemployed again, and again I found another job. I was opening a franchise. But alas, that was not to be either.

So this new failure of closing my business was a severe blow. I had lost all confidence in myself, so I surrendered. My wife was the only thing that kept me from wishing for the end like last time. I could not let her down, so I gave everything I was to God. I would do whatever he asked of me—no matter what it was.

That was about the time I heard God's word of caution about being careful with what I ask for.

And then the music began.

Music

Have you ever lived in an apartment and heard your neighbor's television or stereo when it was too loud? Have you ever lived in a neighborhood and had someone down the street throw a party where you could hear their music? Have you ever lived on a busy street and heard the radios of cars in traffic? Most of us have had an experience like this at one point or another. Some of us have been on the other side of the issue and were ourselves the noisy ones.

What did you hear? How did the music sound to you? Was it crisp and clear? Did you hear a thumping of the bass? Usually the sound we hear the most is the bass because the sound waves of the lower tomes travel the farthest. Normally the source of this music is easy to locate. You can hear it better through a window or your wall is rattling with the thumping of the music. What do you do when you cannot, for the life of you, find the source?

At night when my wife, Kelly, and I lay down to go to sleep, we can hear music. The music is soft and quiet. It is quite easy to miss. When I first began hearing music, my thoughts immediately went to the surrounding area of my house and neighborhood. The back of my house faces a busy street, so that must be considered. Across that busy street is a gas station. That must also be considered. You can hear the music from the cars at the traffic light on the street. That thumping bass was normally what we heard. Only from car radios that are extremely loud can sounds other than bass be heard. Even then, the sounds were loud and very distinct. So after careful consideration, I excluded those sounds.

The music across the street at the gas station was a possibility, but the same problem exists. Deeper sounds travel farther, so any sounds heard would be distorted. The music we hear is smooth and even. It was just extremely faint. I considered the possibility that it was my next-door neighbor. I even went outside and stood next to my neighbor's house to identify the culprit, but once outside, the sounds of music were gone completely and not louder as I had anticipated.

My wife and I would often try to identify the music. Sometimes it was big-band music or classical. Other times the music we heard would be rock and roll. My wife tends to fall asleep pretty quickly, so for her, it was just an odd occurrence and nothing that warranted any special attention. She would tend to ignore these sounds and fall right asleep. As I am sure you can understand, I have had difficulty getting right to sleep for quite a few years now. As a result, I tended to have more time to listen, so I would try to focus on the music and concentrate on identifying it or hearing it better.

In hindsight, this was a *bad* idea, but you probably figured that out for yourself by now. So, there I would lie and listen to the faint music. I would try to figure out what band it was. Sometimes I would figure it out; other times, I would listen and have no idea.

Are you old enough to remember *Name That Tune*? If you do remember, then it was a bit like that except it played constantly. If you are too young to remember, it's probably just as well. The point is the music played, and I listened. What else did I have to do right?

Sleep?

Sure thing—no problem.

Eventually I would drift off to sleep. The next night, it would all begin again.

One night, several months later, I heard a song that I knew rather well. The song that I heard did not play start to finish. It was not a variety of songs I heard. I heard one song. It did not play and repeat. It played only bits and pieces of the song and played them continuously for as long as I was listening. This was the moment when I knew beyond a doubt that the music was not from my neighborhood. This music was clearly from somewhere else entirely.

Every night, the music would play. It would be playing when I went to bed. It would be playing if I woke up in the night. When my alarm would go off in the morning, I could no longer hear the music—but sure enough, it came back each and every night.

Hearing music that had no source was frustrating. More than that, though, it was maddening. It was like a puzzle that I could not solve. With no solution to this puzzle in sight, I eventually learned to ignore the music. I would notice that it was there, but no longer did I care what it was or where it was coming from. It would be enough for me to notice that it was still playing. Then I would pay it no more attention. It was difficult enough for me to fall asleep without making things worse by trying to figure it out. With my newfound determination and sense of purpose, I would lie down for bed and actually try to fall asleep.

That was until the music was accompanied by voices.

Voices

The first voice I heard was maybe two and a half years ago, but before that, other strange things had happened around my house. When you add music and voices, I was convinced my house was haunted. Several occurrences had taken place in early 2013 that were both alarming and fascinating at the same time.

What follows is a record of what happened in the days and months since.

Saturday, February 16, 2013, 6:00 a.m.

I was trying to decide if I was ready to get out of bed or not. Kelly was still sleeping. I had already snoozed the alarm clock and was just working up the energy to haul myself out of bed. Then I heard a voice say, "Thanks for the pile of crap, Uncle Jeff." The "pile of crap" part is what it sounded like. It could have been something else. The other parts were very clear.

Saturday, February 16, 2013, 7:00 p.m.

Kelly had a load of clothes in the drier and a small load of whites in the washer. The drier had been finished for a while, so she added the whites to freshen the wrinkled clothes in the drier. She started the drier and started the water for the washer. While getting the next load, the dryer stopped. She went back in with new load, and the drier door was open.

Date unknown, mid-2013, afternoon

Kelly had been missing an earring. It had been missing for quite some time. One day we walked into the bedroom, and on the comforter in the middle of the bed was the earring.

Date unknown, mid-2013, 5:00 a.m.

Kelly and I were in bed. Kelly was sleeping. Jeff was lying in bed not able to sleep. Light from the street light was illuminating the room slightly. Jeff heard a noise by Kelly's nightstand. Sitting up on an elbow, Jeff looks at Kelly's nightstand and sees a water bottle falling over with a dark shadowy hand catching the bottle and putting it back on the stand.

Sometime around August 2013, 11:00 a.m.

It was around noon on a weekday. Kelly was at work. I do not remember if it was my day off or if it was a few months before that when I was between jobs. Anyway, I was in the living room and was going through Netflix on my TV, browsing for something that catches my eye. I heard a loud and clear voice say, "*Jeff!*" It was fairly loud but was still a whisper. I was alone in the house with the exception of my cat, and unless she suddenly learned to speak, I am fairly certain that it was not her. I looked at my phone, wondering if there was something that could have called my name. The screen was blank. No calls, no texts, no apps or programs open. My laptop was open, but all programs were closed except for a program with my resume on it. The volume of the speaker was turned off. The television was on a menu for Netflix. There was no audio to be heard.

So, what is left?

The only other option I had was that it was a ghost. No need to laugh—I am quite serious. This was quite different from music in the middle of the night. This was 1:30 in the afternoon. The house was silent, which made the call seemed that much louder.

I got up from my seat and walked around the room. Maybe I have seen too many movies. I looked at everything in the room. No electronics other than what I have already mentioned. No hidden speakers. No hidden cameras. There was no one outside. My search spread out from the living room toward the rest of the house. I was still trying to convince myself that it was not a ghost, but my search turned up no clues. The more I looked, the less I found.

There was nothing there.

Maybe I was imagining things. That is entirely possible. That was probably a more favorable option than the alternative ghost theory. But as much as I would have wished otherwise, the voice was quite real. Once you come to the conclusion that it was real and not imagined is when the anxiety increases.

So, a voice calls out to me in the middle of the afternoon, in the middle of my living room, with no one there.

What else could I possibly say to that? Not much. I couldn't just sit there either, so I got up, took a shower, and made myself busy by cleaning the kitchen and mowing the yard. I was reluctant to go back to the living room—the scene of the crime as it were. My laptop was powered off as was the television.

I could not sit still for very long for the rest of the day. When Kelly got home from work, I said nothing. I am not sure why. We both heard the music. Why would a voice from nowhere be unusual? The truth is the thought of telling someone about this would make me sound crazy. That is a pretty short leap, isn't it? I mean after all that has been happening, it would be a reasonable conclusion to say that I was losing my mind.

But that lone voice in the living room was not the last, so I began to document everything that had been happening. I figured it only makes sense, right? If I do lose my marbles, maybe this will help the good doctors understand my journey off the deep end.

Wednesday, January 7, 2014, early a.m.

Woke up in the middle of the night. I heard a very faint voice. Usually it is music. This time it was a voice. Although the voice was very faint, it was shouting, almost screaming, "Grandma! Grandma!" over and over again. I had to focus on noise from the fans and the street to distract me from the voice.

Sometime near the end of January 2014, 5:00 a.m.

I was wake and dreading the day ahead. Here I am, unemployed again, struggling to get by. I am filled with thoughts about how I am going to provide for my wife and give her the kind of life she deserves. It had been a week or two since the voice in the living room. As each day went by, the event slowly faded into a memory. It was the kind of memory that you look back on and wonder if it really happened. But one thing I knew for certain—I was still unemployed, still struggling to get through each day. I lie here and wonder how long my wife will stay with me if I am just an unemployed bum. As I lay there in bed, staring at the ceiling, a voice whispered, "Jeff, do not be afraid. Everything will be all right."

This sounded like a message from God giving me the reassurance that it will all work out. This seemed to be very clear. But again, I wonder whom this kind voice belonged to. Is it a ghost, an angel, or something else that I don't yet understand?

This was, at least, not like the dreams that were so frightening. It was a kind and soothing message that I needed to hear, no doubt, but I could still not mention anything to Kelly. I still feel like I am going crazy—another day, another step closer to the edge of the deep end.

Whoever the voice was from, I took reassurance that things would turn out all right. Although I am still unemployed, today was a better day.

Wednesday, February 26, 2014, sometime between 1:00 a.m. and 4:00 a.m.

I had been having trouble sleeping all night. I think it has been a week or two since the last voices I heard, so that was not what had been keeping me from the precious sleep I wanted and needed. When I had lain down, my eye was a little irritated. Usually if you can leave it alone for a few minutes, your eye will water, and it will start to feel better. The more you rub it, the worse it feels. So, I left it alone, but it did not get any better. It felt like I had something in my eye, and for the life of me, I could not get comfortable. Finally, with sleep nothing more than a fond idea, I got out of bed and searched for a bottle of eye drops. A few eye drops later and my eye still bothering me, I tossed and turned. I'm sure I dozed a little in between the tossing and turning. What seemed like an eternity later, it was now early in the day, sometime before 4:00 a.m., and my frustration was steadily mounting. It surprises me how the more tired I get, the more violent the act of rolling over becomes. When you roll, you punch your pillow and throw the blankets around. Everything has a harsher edge to it. I finally settle a bit and try to calm my breathing. Then, once again, I heard the voice.

She said, "Look at him. He is so tired."

A male voice responded. It was a deep and commanding tone that sounded much harsher than the soft voice she used. I could not understand what he said.

She replied, "It was my pleasure," or "You are quite welcome." I can't remember which. With that voice echoing in my head, I finally fell asleep.

Friday, February 28, 2014, 3:35 a.m.

When I first went to bed last night, I had been thinking about the voices that I hear. I said a short prayer: "Lord, let me know what this stuff means. I wonder who the voice is."

Generally speaking, hearing voices is bad. I have surrendered my life to Christ. The voices must be connected to God somehow. I believe that. I just have no idea how. In time, I am sure God will let me know what this all means.

With these thoughts floating through my mind, I drifted off to sleep.

I had another dream. In the dream, I remember asking, "Who are you?"

A voice said back to me, "My name is Amanda."

In the dream, I was with a friend of mine, a woman (who I do not know). I got separated from my friend and met Amanda. She said I had asked for help, and so she was here to help. She said she has been here for a while. She told me that I could be wearing a ring that had been in her family for years and not realize it. It seemed as though she was implying that we were connected through the ring, but I have no ring other than my wedding ring, and that, to my knowledge, is not that old. As we continued talking, she began to work with a small ring. It looked like a wedding band. The band was about half the size of my pinky. I was writing in a book and could not read the words I was writing. After some time, the page in the book was covered with a square with small zigzag patterns throughout. It covered the whole page except for the margins on both sides as well as the top and bottom. Amanda placed the ring, which at this point looked wet with blood—at least it looked like blood. I can't be certain either way. She told me to take the ring and put it on. I told her I wasn't sure and I didn't want to. I closed the book and went back to where my friend was. I showed her the page in the book and told her about Amanda. We turned to start walking away. We heard a sound and looked back. There had been a small metal table or shelf against the wall behind us. It had a bright silver finish. It began to unfold from the wall. Growing with each movement, it continued to unfold, growing into what looked like a creepy face with metallic teeth. It continued to move closer, faster with each move. As it got closer, we began to run with it lurching to chase after us.

End of dream.

And now for the beginning of the strange part. Yep, as strange as that was, it was nothing compared to what happened next.

I awoke with a little jump. My eyes were heavy and trying to blink myself into understanding of what my dream meant. The quiet voice that I heard said softly, "Jeffrey, it's not real. Go back to sleep."

Yeah, right. Back to sleep. No problem. Then I *thought* to myself I need to look up that name. You see, I put that in italics because I wanted to emphasize the fact that I spoke nothing out loud. Immediately, the soft voice began to say over and over, *"Do not look up Amanda!"* She wasn't really shouting, but there was an urgent and important tone.

So here I am sitting on the couch in my living room typing away at this *thing*—whatever it may be. I do not know whether it is a journal or a book. For now, it is an outlet. I have no idea what direction this is going. I suppose I am just going along for the ride. By the way, I have not (nor will I) looked up Amanda.

It is 4:40 a.m. I am really tired and will try to get a catnap in before I get up to make coffee and breakfast for Kelly before she goes to work.

Saturday, March 1, 2014, 3:30 a.m.

I heard her voice again. This time she simply said, "Jeffrey, believe." Throughout the next couple of hours, each time I would wake up, I would hear, "Believe in me," repeated over and over. And for the first time, when I woke up at 3:30, I heard her voice as I walked throughout the house. I thought I heard a few other things, but the sound was so quiet at times that I could not understand it. I wish she could turn up the volume.

Author/readers' note: Once again, that note of caution that God spoke to me, "Be careful what you ask for"—you will under-stand what I am talking about very soon.

I notice that when I first wake up, it seems the loudest. If I become fully awake and get up for some reason, it will be extremely quiet and will take time for me to adjust and start hearing the voice more clearly. I have even begun to respond (quietly, so I don't wake up my wife)—like last night when she asked, "Do you believe?" and I would whisper "yes" back.

I think the biggest problem I have is that I still don't know who she is. Of course, I believe. I hear her nearly every night now. To me, it is no longer a matter of belief. It is a matter of understanding. I am very detail oriented and ask many questions when faced with something I do not understand—and *this* is something that I do not understand. There is never anything threatening, only a quiet reassurance.

There is a bit of eagerness and excitement to this for me. I cannot explain it. For the first time in my life, I feel like there is something out there; but at the same time, there is a nervous uneasiness. Something is just not quite right.

Sunday, March 2, 2014, 4:15 a.m.

"What do you want me to do? I can't hear you." Those are the words that started my day—but those were not her words. Those were my words. Let me start at the beginning of my night. Shortly after I went to bed, I heard music. Hearing music is a very frequent occurrence. It continued for quite some time. Eventually, I heard that very faint voice.

"Jeff, can you hear me?"

Well, a little, but not very well. That was it until I fell asleep. But just when I thought my life was weird enough, I woke up and tossed and turned briefly at 4:15. Now I hear the voice loud and clear—well, in a whispering kind of way anyway. This time she said, "Jeff, go into the living room."

What? Go into the living room. Loud and clear or not, I must have missed something, so I stayed in bed, listening.

Apparently staying in bed was not the right choice. I heard her say again, "Jeff, go into the living room." So I got up and went into my living room.

Ooh, maybe she will show me something, I thought.

I look around and take an account of the room. TV—check. Couch—check. Fireplace—check. Next to the couch is a stand with my laptop on it. Off to the left is my dining room table. Any ghostly appearances in view? Nope, nothing. I thought it would be easier to hear her in the living room, but *no*, I can't seem to hear anything out here. Well, no appearances evidently.

Then I hear, "Open the laptop."

Okay, gotcha. Laptop open.

Then I sit there like a boob, expecting my laptop to do something. Running out of ideas, I thought back to all those movies I had seen where people communicate with otherworldly people. So I typed those words: "What do you want me to do?" but I can't hear a thing except the cat purring next to me.

Nothing.

I hear "laptop" again and thought she told me to close the laptop.

What? Close it? I just opened it. Now I have a voice playing games with me at 4:30 in the morning. Still, I can't really hear anything, so I close the lid and go back to bed.

Again, it was the wrong choice. "Jeff, go back into the living room now."

Seriously? Fine, I will go out and try it again. I sit on the couch listening. I hear the word *laptop* again. I open the lid. I close the lid. I open the lid and close it again. I am still not hearing anything clearly. Giving up, I go back to bed. This is where is gets weird. As if it wasn't already, right? Try going back to sleep with a voice saying, "Go back into the living room," over and over again. The good news is I did fall back asleep.

"Jeff, go back into the living room."

Oh dear God, really—again? I glance at the clock and see it is seven in the morning.

I have to hand it to her—she is persistent.

"Jeff, go back into the living room and work on your book."

Now all the laptop openings and closings make a little more sense. *She* wasn't the one who was supposed to use it. *I* was. Giving in, I got up and got dressed, made coffee, and sat down at my laptop. The last voice I heard before I started typing was "Jeffrey, go tell the world."

By the way, after reading this, my wife has officially given me notice that if I start acting weird(er), she is going to call a padded truck and check me in.

No pressure.

Monday, March 3, 2014, 4:15 a.m.

Wow, what a difference a day makes.

Today things began to take a disturbing turn—disturbing as in bad.

The thought that has been going on in my head constantly has been that I have got to be losing my mind. Music was easier to deal with because Kelly could hear that as well, but now that it is a voice telling me what to do, it is a completely different story.

How many serial killers have said they have done horrible things because voices tell them to? She has done nothing to harm me or tell me anything bad yet, but who is she? What does she want?

So, in an effort to either confirm or deny my sanity, I have decided to try and record the voices. I am not sure how it will go or if I will even capture anything. I have been looking for a recorder of some kind but am in no position to spend the money. I will just have to use the voice recorder function on my phone and hope for the best although to be completely honest, I am not sure what "hoping for the best" even means anymore.

I just hope I am not going mad.

First recording

It is now about 10:00 a.m., and I have tried to find a quiet room in the house with the least amount of noise or distractions. After sitting in my living room, it was very difficult to hear. I was not hopeful of hearing anything out there, so I go into the bathroom/ laundry room. It is the only room in the house without windows. It is also a room that I can close the doors to completely shut myself off from any outside noise.

I start by just sitting and listening. You have to adjust to the silence and focus on hearing the smallest of sounds. It is much like your eyes adjusting to the darkness. It takes a few minutes before you can see anything, and in that same way, it takes time to adjust. I turn on the recorder and just listen.

Then I begin to ask questions.

"Who are you?"

"What do you want?"

I heard my name called out several times. It seemed like my name was being called by different voices. I also heard more about telling the world and writing my book. I could hear more being said in the background, but the words were faint and hard to understand in the playback on my phone. I played the recording several times. I would listen to short moments were voices could be heard over and over. Sometimes I would pick up words, and sometimes I would hear an unintelligible voice.

I would have to download the recordings to my laptop if I want to be able to hear anything better. I would not know anything else until I could listen to the recordings. One thing was clear—the voices were real, and they were calling my name.

Tuesday, March 4, 2014, early morning

It was another night of voices calling me to go and write my book. The voices I heard were many. As usual, there was the soft voice that continued to call to me, but there were more. There was the deep and gruff voice in the background. He was talking to the woman with the soft voice. There was also what sounded like screaming.

This was when things got truly frightening. After all of my nightmares, I am not as easy to scare as I used to be, but this was different. The voices I heard were louder than before—almost like they were in the room with me. I wanted desperately to understand what was happening. I prayed that God would help me figure out what was going on. The more I heard, the less I trusted the voices. I wanted and needed to know for sure. I did not want to blindly follow something that I did not fully understand.

Second recording

I found some headphones that I could plug into my phone so I could hear what was being said a bit more clearly. I sat down in the quietest place I could find and relistened to yesterdays' recordings. In the recordings, I could hear the woman's voice and the deep voice of the male spirit. I call it a spirit because at this point, I really do not know what it is. I do get a very clear sense that it is not a good thing. I also heard another voice that was screaming my name followed by other unintelligible words.

I sat down again with my phone and began asking questions.

"Who are you?"

"What do you want from me?"

"What book do you want me to write? What is this book supposed to be about?"

"You have been kind to me so far. I just need to know more."

I listened again with the headphones and the phone. I heard the same voices I heard last time. I also heard very deep sounds and more sounds that sounded angry. It was like they were being played on fast forward and I could not understand them. There was more screaming and many other sounds that I could not identify.

I finally decided that the phone was not enough for me to understand much of anything. Listening to the sounds on the phone was definitely enough for me to realize that they were real and I was not imagining them. So, I decided to copy the recordings from my phone to my laptop.

On my laptop, I had a program that let me do some video editing. It allowed me to slow down the portions of the recordings that sounded too fast for me to understand. I was also hopeful I could filter out some of the static that you hear when listening to music at too high a volume.

It took me quite some time to get the audio recordings loaded on my laptop. I only had a short time to listen to them that day. All I really accomplished today was to figure out how to slow down the playback and filter some of the noise. Even though the spot I was sitting was very quiet, it was surprising how loud all the background noises became once I turned the volume up high enough to hear some of the other voices. It was not too complicated to figure things out, but anything else would have to wait until tomorrow.

Wednesday, March 5, 2014, early morning

The playback

I decided to spend some more time reviewing the recordings today. Listening to them yesterday made me a little uncomfortable, so I was hesitant to listen to them today, but it is too late for me to be skittish. I have gone too far to just stop. I need more answers.

As I just typed that last sentence, it hit me how ridiculous that sounds. More answers would imply that I have some already and just need a bit more. The reality is the only thing I have found so far at all is confusion topped off by a very uneasy feeling. I have no more answers than I did when this whole thing started.

Well, I did learn that I was not crazy, but can you really say at this point that that is a good thing?

Me neither.

So, here I sit, laptop opened and ready, headphones ready. That uneasy feeling is still there, but I need to finish this and be done with it. I can't look back and wonder what it said. I am thinking that I need to finish what I started, but I have a feeling that this is not the end of anything, only the beginning.

I head to the first portion of the recording that I have selected to review.

"I know you are there. Say something. You have only been kind to me."

The deep voice that I have heard before began to laugh a deep and menacing laugh.

"He is ours now!"

More evil laughing, screaming, followed by a voice calling my name and saying, "Help me."

Okay, this is downright creepy. I slow the recording down and listen to it again.

"Uncle Jeff! Help me! They are hurting me! Uncle Jeff, please help me and write your book!"

This was followed by more screaming.

I hit Stop and yanked the headphones and threw them to the table. My heart was racing. Fear was rising up in me to the point where my hands were shaking.

That was the voice of my nephew Matthew. Fear and doubt were everywhere before me. Everything I thought I believed in was suddenly called into question. Whoever these spirits were, they were definitely not good. They were no messengers of God—I am pretty sure of that.

But what book are they talking about? I still do not know who they are, but I believe in God. I know my nephew was a Christian, so that could not have been him. The strange thing that happened as I sat and stared at my headphones next to the laptop, my thoughts were centered on Matt. A calm reassurance filled me with a sense that I knew that the voice of my nephew was a lie. It was a lie that was told with a singular purpose—to fill me with fear.

It worked. Even though I knew it was a lie, it still worked. The fear was very real.

I gather my senses and put the headphones back on.

I went to another portion of the recording.

"What do you want from me?"

"Jeff, you have to finish your book. You have to tell the world."

I heard the part about "tell the world" clear enough on the phone, but it was not until now that I heard the whole sentence.

"Tell the world what?"

"That God is not real."

This sent a wave of panic through me—not that I doubted God's existence but because I began to piece together who these voices might belong to.

"Who are you?"

"Satan."

"What do you want from me?"

"I want you to die!"

Oh hell no. I slammed the laptop shut and yanked the headphones from my ears. My breathing was heavy, and my heart pounded. Sweat was pouring from my face.

This was bad. This was very bad.

Was this how Pandora felt when she opened her box? This wasn't just bad; it was profoundly bad. There are not enough adjectives to describe how bad this was.

There on a recording on my laptop was a voice who claimed to be Satan telling me he wanted me to die.

How bad could it be? Really?

What echoed in my mind were the first words I heard from God: "Jeff, be careful what you ask for."

Suddenly I felt like the foolish child who when he meets God for the first time tells him to prove it.

What have I gotten myself into? Wasn't my life complicated enough already? Didn't I have enough to worry about?

Jeffrey, you are a damned fool, I thought to myself.

Thursday, March 6, 2014, early morning

How do you think I slept last night? I bet you thought I would fall right asleep and dream of bunny rabbits and ice cream cones.

You know me better than that by now, don't you? Needless to say, sleeping was a difficult thing to master. No sooner had I laid my head down upon my pillow than the voices began.

The soft voice of the woman was gone. She had done her job, I suppose. She had gotten me sucked into this madness and moved on to other things. I wonder if she got a pat on the back and a few days off for her good work.

"Jeff, you're gonna die!"

There were several voices that repeated this for the duration of the night. I tried to bury my head in the pillow and cover my ears with the covers. These voices were not in my head; they were there in the room with me, shouting as I tried to sleep. I glanced over at my wife on several occasions to make sure she didn't hear anything and thankful that she remained deep asleep.

"*Jeff, you are going to die!*"

I cannot call them voices. I know exactly what they are. It is as clear as if they had been wearing a name tag that says, "Hi, my name is…"

They were not ghosts or just voices from the other side. These were demons and the evil spirits that do their bidding. There was no mistaking it.

Again, I chastised myself for getting into this mess in the first place: "If you hear a creepy voice, don't listen. If you meet God, you don't ask him to prove it."

In the morning, I went outside of the house with my phone in my hand. Somehow, being outside the house felt safer. I am not sure why. It would only make sense that demons could follow you outside and torment you just as easily as they could inside. When I got to the driveway, I opened my phone and called my mother. My mother is the person at church who coordinates prayers when people need them. She has a vast network of prayer warriors who vigilantly pray for those in need. In her experience, she has faced many things, demons included. She prayed for me over the phone and had some other people pray for me as well. I felt better, but I was still terrified of what I had started.

I called the church today and made an appointment to meet with my pastor. I am hoping that he will be able to help.

Friday, March 7, 2014, early morning

Once again, sleeping is difficult to find. What I do find is fitful and unproductive. I wake in the morning feeling like I had hardly slept at all. The demons and spirits continued to shout at me all night.

"You're sick. You are going to go to the hospital tomorrow and will die. You will leave your wife all alone."

They have become so loud that I have been unable to block them or tune them out. It is starting to get unbearable. I bury my head underneath the covers and hold my hands over my ears to try to block them. Not surprisingly, it does not work.

My anxiety continues to build.

Sunday, March 9, 2014, early morning

For the past three days, I have heard the demons torment me with predictions of my death. I have grown so weary of it that I dread to go to sleep. There is never any rest or comfort to be found, only torment and anger and hostility.

"Jeff, you are sick and are going to die. You should have just written the book."

More evil laughing.

What have I done?

I wanted answers.

I got answers. There were not the ones I wanted or expected, but I got them.

I used to feel alone and longed for someone or something to be there.

Now, I wished that I was alone. I did not want to hear any voices. I wish I could take back all of the things that I did to start this mess. I feared not for myself but for my wife. In what way would she have to pay for my foolishness?

Lord, I am sorry for what I have done. Please forgive me for starting this. Please, Lord, make it stop.

My wife and I went to church today. I felt better. While I was in those walls, I felt protected. I felt safe.

That safety and security was short-lived. As the sun began to fade, the fear and apprehension began to fill me with dread.

Even with nightmares, I still felt like going to sleep was a good thing. It was refreshing to curl up in bed as sleep drifted in. I was used to the nightmares. They were weird and horrible, but I was used to them. They did not bother me. Now, the thought of going to sleep filled me with anxiety.

Monday, March 10, 2014, early morning

Another night of torment. I put on some earplugs and hope that it would allow me a moment's peace. To my surprise, the voices were quieter when I had the earplugs in. It helped, but it was still nearly impossible to get a good night's sleep.

I continue to hear the voices tell me that I am going to die. They are continuing to use everything they can to fill me with fear.

Today I meet with pastor. I am looking forward to hearing what he has to say. All the voices that I am hearing is pure madness. I feel like I am going out of my mind. Just when I think I am okay, the enemy cranks up the volume on the voices. I need this to stop. I am hoping that the pastor, Steve, will be able to help me figure out what to do.

If he believes me, that is. I honestly never thought about that possibility. I wouldn't blame him at all if he thought I was nuts.

What would you think?

I have been in nervous anticipation of meeting with Pastor Steve. My appointment is toward the end of the day, so I have all day to wait.

Finally met with Steve. To my great relief, he believes me. He said it all sounds very demonic and that, for some reason, the demons are targeting me. He listened patiently and asked many questions. Many of the questions were regarding what I had done leading up to the voices. He also asked about how I had been reacting to them. I told him that I had cast them out in the name of Jesus Christ but nothing happened.

He was very concerned and made the recommendation that I go through *deliverance.*

There is only one thing that comes to mind when I think of deliverance. You too, huh? That's right—cue the banjo music.

I like banjos as much as the next guy, but what that has to do with demons tormenting me in my house, I can only imagine.

I was soon to learn that deliverance is an intense focused prayer and counseling session. I was to schedule this as soon as I could.

When I returned home, I made some phone calls and scheduled a meeting with the two-person team that would be conducting my deliverance. An initial meeting was scheduled for Wednesday at 6:00 p.m. Part of me was disappointed that it would not be for another couple of days, but I had been listening to demons for this long, so what would another few days hurt.

Tuesday, March 11, 2014, early morning

When I went to bed last night, the voices picked up right where they had left off. As I have discovered so far, at least my own theory or understanding of it, there are several demons and evil spirits that torment me. The first one was the woman with the soft and smooth voice. I remember the time that a guttural and scary voice that I could not make out spoke to her, and she said, "It was my pleasure." She seems to be entirely different from all the others. In hindsight, her soft and quiet demeanor strikes me as more frightening than the ones that come out and say they will kill me. She was one who had a very clearly defined purpose. It was to lure me in to the waiting trap. Once in, I was passed on to the next crew. To help make things less confusing, I will call her Amanda.

The second distinct type is the one that I hear most often. It makes me think of a juvenile. It repeats what I say word for word in that annoying little brother way. As a little brother myself, I understand this. This entity appears to be charged with getting under my skin and causing me many sleepless nights. They are annoying to the point of no return. So once again, in an effort to make this madness seem a little clearer, I will call this one Little Brother.

And then there are the ones that sound big and scary. When I have a moment of success against one of the others, that deep and menacing voice comes forward. With these, there is no beating around the bush. They are mean, nasty, and pure evil. Although I realize that it sounds silly, I will call this one Peaches. I don't like peaches, but I mean no offense to the peach-loving world.

If you could possibly have a demon more frightening than that, the one I heard this morning fit the bill. The sound of the voice sent a chill through me and made my skin crawl just by listening to it.

"Jeff, you are going to die and be by my side. Ha, ha, ha."

As it seems to be forming a pattern, I usually hear the scary ones when I have done something right, so deliverance must be a very important step in the right direction. All I can do is wait for the meeting tomorrow.

Deliverance

Wednesday, March 12, 2014, 6:00 p.m.

Last night brought more of the same torment. There was a mix of annoying demons and spirits along with the big scary ones thrown in for good measure. I am very hopeful that the prayer team can help rid me of these demons. I am at a loss to explain why they have chosen me to torment. I am equally at a loss to explain why God has chosen to let this happen.

Now before you get britches in a bunch, let me explain. Christ said that if you cast them out in his name, they *must* obey. Am I doing it wrong? Is it only for people who meet a certain level of faith? Or is it only for people who have been believers for a certain number of years? It must be something because I have cast them out every night for a week, and nothing has happened. I have heard many stories of people casting out demons in the name of Jesus Christ, and immediately the demons flee. What am I doing wrong?

The two people who would be conducting the deliverance sessions arrived a short time before six. We walked through the house briefly before sitting down in the living room. I gave them a brief but detailed explanation of what had been happening. They asked many questions. Many of the questions were similar to those asked by Pastor Steve.

There was never a doubt in their voices. They shared some of the experiences they have had in the past with matters like these. There was even an instance where a demon had hurled a Bible at them while they were praying for someone. They had many years of experience in dealing with demons and torments like mine.

They also asked me what I said when I cast out the demons. They explained how this might not even be about me specifically. The Bible talks of curses being passed down several generations. We prayed and talked for nearly an hour.

They wanted to meet with me again on Friday. That would be our first official session.

Friday, March 14, 2014, 6:00 p.m.

Prayer time. I met again with Pam and Henry. We began with an update of how things had been going for the past couple of days. We went over the topics we had discussed on Wednesday and covered each item in greater detail. Every topic was prayed about. They also asked other more specific questions. These were questions about any experiences I may or may not have had with the occult. There were also questions about my heritage.

Friday, March 21, 2014, weekly update

Mostly quiet since the deliverance meeting. Quiet voices. On Monday, Kelly and I sang a praise and worship song before bed. No voices at all.

Wednesday

"Jeff, you're gonna die! Jeff, you're gonna die!"
On the third time, I interrupted him.
"Jeff, you're gonna—"
"Live forever!"
"Jeff, you're gonna—"
"Have everlasting life!"
No more voices that night.

Thursday

"Jeff, I'm the devil. Come out and play?" It was a little different than before; it was deep and menacing.

"Bite him! Bite him! (more than one voice)"

"Jeff… Jeff…"

"You're gonna die."

God, why are you teaching me to hear demons?

I heard a response almost immediately.

"Jeffrey, I am not teaching you to hear demons. I am teaching you to hear me."

This response was far different than any of the voices I had heard so far. This was inside my head—but not simply a voice. It was a thought that was carefully placed in my head while at the same time an audible sound. The only way I can explain it is like subtitles. It was a thought, a sound, and a feeling all at the same time, and there was no mistaking the source. This was God. It was full of compassion and comfort. It was the voice of a father speaking to a frightened child, but it was also the voice of a teacher guiding a student. It was stern and direct but filled with love. I could feel the love in the words as I heard them.

This was a very powerful experience for me. It let me know that there is purpose to what is happening. I no longer have a feeling of being cursed or condemned to a future of torment. Although it is still an uncertain future, at least I know now that God is trying to teach me something. Whatever he is trying to teach me remains elusive. I see no direction for this newfound training.

Looking back at where this whole thing started, I asked him to show me he was real. He did—in a major way. I also told him that I would do whatever he asked. So, on we go with the torment of demons. Only God knows the plan. I just have to try and deal with what he gives me. I have faith that he will never abandon me, but that in itself does not ease the feelings of torment and fear that I face on a nightly basis. In the book of Job, God allows Satan to make Job suffer. There were conditions to this suffering. Satan was not allowed to harm Job, but in reading the book, Job suffered greatly.

To be clear, I do not think I am walking a path similar to Job. In my gut, I believe that God has a plan for what he is teaching me. I will do whatever he asks of me, but that is not a guarantee that whatever I face will come without cost. That cost could be in the form of torment and fear. The cost could be much greater. I must have faith.

Saturday

Wow! I am not even sure how to begin this part. Once we started the deliverance process, the voices started getting better. Thursday was a bit of a downturn. Friday was a bit of the same. But this morning (Saturday) was a whole new world of emotions. I went to bed a bit late last night and fell asleep rather quickly. It is fairly typical for me to wake up and roll over around 3:30 to 4:00 a.m. That is why I hear things at this time more frequently than any other.

The first thing I heard was "Let me in." It was so real that I actually got up to check outside to see if someone was there. With the neighborhood looking peaceful and quiet, I headed back to the bedroom. I then heard the voice a bit more clearly. It was that same deep, gravely, and almost growling voice that spoke. Its words were haunting as it said, "Jeff, let me in."

"Let me in!"

"Let me in!"

"Let me in!"

To be perfectly honest, the first thing I thought of was the movie *The Exorcist*. So when it said, "Let me in," I, of course, started thinking of possession. That was not merely scary but terrifying. This was one of the first times that the fear had been that great. I immediately started reciting every prayer I knew. I began singing all the praise and worship songs I could think of. What made it the scariest was my uncontrollable need to say "come in." I did not want to say it, but it was there, wanting to jump out of my mouth. So I did, but I followed it with "to my life and my soul, Lord Jesus."

After struggling with this for about a half hour, the voice began saying, "Let me out of your heart and into your mind."

Oh damn! Did I let the enemy in? Why did I do that? How did I do that? Just at that moment, a soft and loving voice said, "It is because you are afraid."

Oh, okay, gotcha—but still what do I do now?

About another half hour later, I decided to get up and grab my iPhone. I went out to the living room and grabbed my phone. I pushed the button on the phone and used the light from the screen to look around for a pair of headphones that I was sure was here somewhere. Finding the headphones, I headed back to bed. Kelly woke up and asked if it was the voices again. She said I should tell them to leave in Jesus's name, so we did. We then said a short prayer, and I went to sleep after another twenty minutes or so. I slept for about an hour, struggling to get comfortable, sleeping with headphones on. I did feel better and was still singing songs and praying in my head. I decided to put the earplugs in so I could tune out the voices a little easier and went back to sleep.

I woke up again about 7:30, and things changed again. This time I was not sure what to make of it at all. The voice was there. It was loud. It was as loud as a faint voice could possibly get. Normally I have to tune out the noises around me and really listen. This time, I could hear it above noises emerging from outside. I could hear it above the noise of the fan in the room. It was screaming at me. I decided to get up, and for the first time, I could hear the scream as I walked around the house and made coffee. Over and over it screamed, "GET OUT OF MY HEAD! GET OUT OF MY HEAD! GET OUT OF MY HEAD!"

I could almost picture a big scary demon with my voice whispering softly in his head, "Our Father, who art in heaven…"

Is it wrong for me to want to laugh?

Sunday—"Welcome to living with the world of the dead."

Tuesday—"You're not alive. You are like peanut butter."

This was Little Brother again. Doesn't he sound like a ten-year-old?

PART 2
A Glimmer of Light

Newfound Strength

Late spring, 2014

I am beginning to see how God will never give you more than you can handle. Every time I get hit with something that puts my fear and anxiety to an all-new high, he gives me some kind of reassurance that he will not leave me.

From time to time, however, my strength and faith are tested. This morning I woke up and began my normal routine. I tried to document any new events of the voices. It can be quite repetitive if they continue to say the same things as always. Once Kelly woke up, we sat down for coffee, and she told me what I was most afraid to hear. Last night, for a brief moment, she heard voices too.

It is one thing to torment me. I can handle it. I have become quite accustomed to fear and torment, but to have Kelly face a similar torment was unbearable. I tried my best to conceal my fear and told her to try her best to ignore the voices. Sing praise and worship until you fall asleep. She assured me that she would. I felt better knowing that she would not be as foolish as I had been. She would not try to figure out who and what they were. She is much smarter than I was.

As the day wore on and night drew closer, my fear and anxiety began to build. As we lay down to go to sleep, we said our nightly prayers. We prayed that God would protect us and watch over us. In my mind, I said a private prayer. My plea to God was that he would spare my beautiful wife. Please God, do not let her suffer the same torments I have.

Kelly quickly fell asleep, and I could hear her quiet snore. A short time later, the voices began. The voice I heard was the demon that is scarier than Peaches. Of all the demons whose torments I hear, his I like the least. It did not take him long to hit me where I most feared.

"Ha, ha, ha. Thank you for giving me your wife. Ha, ha, ha."

My fear was beyond measure. That fear lasted, but a split second before, a thought was placed carefully in my mind. Once again, this was a thought that was not mine. Again, it was a thought, a voice, and a feeling all at the same time. It was soft and kind. It had a confidence that I would never have been able to muster on my own. While I was still in awe of what the thought was, the words came out of my mouth: "She is not mine to give."

As I lay in bed with those words barely out of my mouth, a wide smile spread across my face. I knew exactly what those words meant. This message was not meant for me alone. To the demons, whose voices continue to torment me, it was a clear warning—not her. For the purpose of this education that God is providing me, she is off-limits. To me the message was also crystal clear. I could see it as clearly as if I were standing before God himself.

The message for me was twofold. The first was a simple claim of ownership. Kelly, for all the love I have for her, is not my responsibility to protect from evil spirits and demons. She is his to protect. She is his child, and he will protect her better than I ever could. Another way to put it is to say that God has told me, "Jeffrey, you focus on the task that I have set before you. Let *me* worry about the rest."

The second meaning of God's message was this: Why fear? What Christ has said, we have the authority to banish.

> *Look, I have given you authority over all the*
> *power of the enemy, and you can walk among snakes*
> *and scorpions and crush them. Nothing will injure*
> *you. But don't rejoice because evil spirits obey you;*
> *rejoice because your names are registered in heaven.*
> (Luke 10:19)

In the name of Jesus Christ, we have the authority to cast out demons. We have been given authority over them. That is the truth that God has shared with us. It is up to us to remember this truth when we are faced with the attacks of the enemy. The only power the enemy has over us is that which *we* give him.

We have been promised, as believers and followers of Christ, that we shall not perish but have everlasting life (John 3:16). The enemy can still lead us astray—if we let him. That part is up to us. We have the responsibility to use the tools that *he* has given us. The first tool that *he* has given us to use is truth. The truth will set you free (John 8:32).

This was a major turning point for me. The fear that has been plaguing me is beginning to wane. My confidence begins to grow. With that confidence, my faith is beginning to grow. It is faith that God is real. It is faith that God is really there. It is faith that God will never abandon us. It is also faith that God has a plan.

Whatever direction and purpose he has in this, I will go where he calls.

When *he* calls you, what will your answer be?

Will you step out upon the water?

Early summer of 2014

As I sit here and write, I am not entirely sure how to describe the incident which took place a few short weeks ago. Did God tell the demons that Kelly was not mine to give? Did they recognize it as a message from God? Was it told to me alone? Was the enemy not aware of the message being from God? To be perfectly honest, I am not sure how to describe it; but either way, it has been a few short weeks since then, and the enemy has not mentioned Kelly at all.

They still scream in my ear and tell me I am going to die. It is becoming aggravating more than anything else at this point because they are so loud that falling asleep is still quite difficult. The events of last night give me new confidence that all of that is about to change.

Once again, as Kelly and I lay down for bed, we say our nightly prayers. We asked the Lord to protect us and our home. "Lord, you and your angels are welcome here in our home. We serve you and have faith that you will guide us along your path."

A short time later, I heard the voice of the evil spirit that I have been calling Little Brother. He had come to torment and taunt me for another evening. I have an image of them showing up to my house each evening like they are reporting for work as if there is a demonic time clock on the back fence where they punch in for work each night. When they slip up, their supervisor shows up. Occasionally, the regional manager shows up to lay down the law.

This time he was telling me of how I was going to die tomorrow when all of a sudden, he stopped in midsentence.

"What do you mean I am not allowed in the house! I have to go in the house!"

Short pause.

"So be it. He can still hear me from the window!"

Another short pause.

"What! I am not allowed outside the window either?"

Another short pause.

"I will go around front! He will hear me from there!"

Another short pause.

"*What?* I am not allowed in the front either? *Aaarrggghhh!*"

I still heard him that night, but it was much quieter like he was standing in the neighbor's yard, screaming at me from there. For me, this was a miracle of epic proportions. A word from God was all I had ever recognized. By recognize, I mean that he could have been speaking to me and showing me miracles for ages only to have me too distracted to notice. There was a miracle in my past though. That was when I met my wife, but I am starting to get off topic. So, the short version. Match.com. First date for both of us. Dessert. Knew we would be married within an hour.

Where was I?

Ah, yes, too distracted to notice anything God had been telling me. Miracle of epic proportions. For me and the limited experience I have had, this was the equivalent of a pillar of fire.

Put it this way—go back and read the events again.

What image comes to your mind when you finish?

For me, the image was larger than life—the evil spirit, minion of the demons who torment me shows up to work for a night of torment to find his favorite haunt closed to him. Standing at the door/window where he enters is an angel. Like a huge bouncer, the angel will not let him enter. More than that, the angel escorts him off the property and tells him he is no longer allowed to enter any closer than where he now stands.

That is how I see it. What else could it be? A sign on the door? That would be okay except for the fact that as he steps back, he finds out that he has not gone far enough. There had to be someone there telling him where to go. I also find it difficult to believe that a demon or evil spirit would be very good at following instructions unless, of course, those instructions came from someone that he had no power to refuse.

If we were to cast out a demon in the name of Jesus Christ, they, of course, leave. From our point of view, the name of Jesus is enough to banish them, and that is true; but I also believe that when we cast out a demon in the name of Jesus Christ, we have the support of God's heavenly army. His angels carry out the command to leave. The name of Christ is enough all by itself. The angels are just there to tell the enemy how far back to stand.

If we have the faith of a mustard seed to tell a mountain it must move, then the mountain will move. To date, none of us has ever moved that mountain, so our faith, no matter how strong, still needs work. It still needs to grow. If we had faith that could move mountains, the angels might not be needed to push the enemy back. But until our faith is strong enough, the angels are there to support us, not just protect us.

God's message of teaching me to hear him is now beginning to make sense. I understand now that even though the voices I heard were those of the enemy, the message I received were from God. I heard demons, but in my mind, I saw the angels that must have been there.

The farther down this road I go, the more I am humbled by whatever plan God must have for my life. The voices, now much more muted, are still there, so I must continue to be vigilant.

Sunday, July 27, 2014

I am still amazed at how much better it is with the voices no longer screaming in my ear. They sound like they are shouting from down the street. That is something that I am very grateful for. It has been much easier for me to tune them out. They are still there. They are persistent—I will give them that. As has become customary, the voices still taunt me with the way I am to die that day.

Last night, a familiar voice returned. It was the same one I first heard. Amanda was back. As always, she is extremely polite and soft-spoken.

"Jeff."

That was all she said, eerily similar to the very first time I heard her call; and as quickly as the voice came, it was gone again.

Monday, July 28, 2014

The larger-than-life scary voice that I have heard on only a few occasions has once again showed up to taunt me. As of yet, I have not given him a name. It feels awkward to give names to them. In a way, it feels wrong—like I am taking them lightly or something. But with so many showing up, I need a way to tell them apart. I am not claiming them like some sort of twisted pet. I do not like them nor do I want them anywhere in my presence. However, God has deemed it necessary that I learn from them. I am still unsure of how this is to unfold, but I accept God's plan and do the best I can.

With all that said, I have come to call this demon the Boss. He only shows up when the others make no progress. I anticipate hearing from him more. I do not plan on letting the others make any progress at all.

"Jeff, you are going to die!"

"You have no power over me but that which I give you," I replied.

"You are wrong!"

"Am I?" Hey, he did tell me I would die "today" every day for the past week.

One of the things I have learned is that Christ has given me and us the authority to cast them out in Jesus's name. They have been banished from my home. Deep down, I know that they can come back in—if I let them. My actions are what can let them back in. I hope I am strong enough to withstand their manipulations.

I must be careful not to get cocky and reckless. It is likely to come back and bite me later on.

Friday, August 1, 2014

Wow, Monday, it was the Boss, and now, it is Peaches again. I must be popular.

"You have no fear of us, so we are going home," he said.

For a brief moment, I was elated. It did not last long. Reality came back to my mind quick enough. There is nothing that they have been truthful about up to this point, so why would they start now?

Only time will tell.

Sunday, August 2, 2014

"Jeff."

Oh, great God in heaven—really? Again? Will they ever leave me alone? I knew the answer to that question before I completed the sentence.

The answer is no. They will not leave me alone. They will never leave us alone. The difference is I can hear them, but they still taunt us all, trying to pull us off course and away from God.

"Jeff."

Yep, she is back.

"What? I don't trust you. You started all this. You opened the door and invited in all those demons and evil spirits that have been tormenting me for months. What are you?"

"I am an angel."

Now she says she is an angel, and she believes that Jesus Christ is the son of God. She even speaks prayers.

"An angel wouldn't whisper to me in the dead of night so I could barely hear."

"I am not whispering. I am shouting across the barrier of the dead."

Okay, that's not creepy at all, is it? Definitely not an angel.

Which is scarier?

Which is scarier? The enemy who says they want you to die, or the enemy who says they love you and are sent by God? Somehow I think that if God sent someone, they would not need to try and convince me of it after they have been hanging out with demons for the last several months—sort of like the dog with the innocent look in its face while your living room is covered in stuffing from your couches and pillows or the child who says they did not eat the candy while their face is covered in chocolate.

I am a firm believer that when God speaks and wants you to know something, you will know it. Whether it is in the form of an angel such as Mary heard tell her she was going to be the mother of the son of God or as the burning bush that Moses saw on the side of the mountain. If he really wants you to know something, there will be no mistaking it. That does not mean that you will always recognize when God is speaking to us. In fact, that is one of the biggest difficulties that Christians face.

The problem so many face is recognizing when God speaks to us. I think he speaks to us often. Sometimes we think it is our own thoughts or ideas. Other times, we completely miss the clues. It is not that he doesn't want us know, nor does he want us to have a difficult time or prove ourselves. On the contrary, he wants us to learn and to grow. He wants us to grow closer to him. He wants our faith and trust to grow, and it grows as we learn. We learn to tell the difference between what he is saying and all of the other outside influences of our lives. We learn to see the miracles around us and beauty that he has given us. We learn, and our faith grows. We learn to trust.

Sometimes that trust is learned the hard way. It is not that he wants to see us struggle. He wants us to depend upon him. When we see how he provides for us and gets us through the difficult times, we learn to see how our prayers are answered. We all struggle with this. I prayed that he would protect my family and my wife. He answered my prayers by forcing the demons from my house and by claiming my wife, Kelly, as his very own.

It is difficult to look at being tormented by demons as anything but bad. possibly even a curse, and I look back to my own pleas to God and wanting nothing more than to know he was real. His response of "be careful what you ask for" brings me back down to earth. Almost like the commercial, he looks down upon me and asks, "Can you hear me now?"

Why yes, sir, I can.

But the things I have gained apart from my own band of demons assigned to my endless torment, I never would have witnessed without them—hearing God say that he is trying to teach me something. It is one thing to make an educated guess that God is trying to teach us something, but to hear him say that he is trying to teach me something—that is beyond anything I could have imagined. To hear the demons as they were evicted from my home was to witness the protection of God over my house. That is a blessing and a gift that I will treasure for the rest of my life.

I do not know for what purpose he is teaching me these things. I can only imagine what that might be. As many sleepless nights as I have had for the past several years now, I am not sure I want to imagine anything. Reality, however difficult it might be to grasp, has proven to be much more terrifying than anything my imagination could have come up with.

Tuesday, August 5, 2014

Another night of voices. Since the deliverance and the banishment from our home, things have been much better. The voices have not stopped as much as I wish they would have, but they have been much more easy to tolerate. Some nights are worse than others. Having demons tell you that you are going to die all the time can wear you down. Not only that, but they frequently tell me to do things. I have heard stories of serial killers who claimed to be doing what the voices had told them to do. I used to think they were lying for the benefit of an insanity defense—either that, or they were just plain crazy.

In all honesty, I have been having second thoughts about that lately. They have told me to kill people, and as much as I have learned throughout this experience, controlling my tongue still has a way to go. One morning, Peaches told me to go to work early to kill someone who usually arrives early. I responded by swearing at him and telling him what he can do.

He laughed at me and said, "Ha, ha, ha! You're not like all the others."

Sorry, Lord. I am still working on that part.

As I think about everything they have been telling me, a thought just occurred to me. These voices have been telling me constantly to work on my book. They want me to tell the world that God is not real. I, of course, have been avoiding writing, so I would not be doing what they want. But what if that is what they want? They have accepted that I have no fear of them. If they had never mentioned writing at all, I would have been feverishly writing all of this. But by telling me to write, I refuse. By that refusal, I think I am doing what they want.

So, I think I need to put more effort into writing all this down.

Friday, August 8, 2014

The voices are still annoying. They are so constant in their taunts that I try to sing music to occupy my mind. If I am busy singing, I won't be paying attention to what they are saying. At this stage in my walk of faith, I still don't know much Christian music, so the songs I have been singing are the ones I know. That is when Little Brother starts repeating the words of the songs I sing. That, of course, is frustrating and annoying beyond belief.

So, I take the high road.

Right?

Come on. I can take the high road. I am capable of taking the high road.

Nope. Not this time.

Sorry, Lord, no high road this time. If an evil spirit wants to pester me with this childish behavior, I can be very childish and immature. This is a game I can play too.

Have you ever wondered what it would sound like for a demon or evil spirit sing the "C Is for Cookie" song?

Yep, me too; and to be perfectly honest, it was pretty funny.

But now I must act like the grown-up and say how foolish this was. I am working on it. Sometimes in frustration I lose control of my sense of judgment. This kind of behavior is tantamount to taunting a demon. Now that sounds like really bad idea, doesn't it?

Well, it is a bad idea. There is nothing in the Bible that tells us to taunt demons. Christ would be disappointed in treating anyone in such a fashion, I think. I will try harder not to get carried away like that again.

As I lay in bed, I try to think of another song to sing, and then I get a brilliant idea.

You could sense the sarcasm there, couldn't you? Not a brilliant idea at all—bad idea if ever there was one—but I will let you be the judge.

In my mind, the fiddle started playing right before Charlie Daniels began to sing. And then "the devil went down to Georgia, looking for a soul to steal."

I am not sure how far I got before I was rudely interrupted by the Big Boss.

"You are an arrogant bastard!"

Yep. I should have seen that coming. "Forgive me, Lord, for being an arrogant fool."

I think that is the first time and only time at this point that I have ever heard a demon speak the truth, and he was furious too—very furious.

It sounds funny now, but the idea of taunting a demon has got to be the dumbest idea I have ever had. They are nothing to be laughed at. They are nothing to underestimate. They are very serious and, as history has shown, very dangerous. Talk about grabbing a tiger by the tail. There is a right way and a wrong way to handle things. I, of course, have done plenty of both, and I sincerely hope you can see the seriousness of the mistakes I have made.

Sunday, August 17, 2014

My wife and I went to church this morning. At one point, I sat and began to pray quietly. I thought of my sister. It occurred to me that she too was facing demons, but she could not hear them as I do. They taunt her, berate her, and tell her how unworthy she is. She cannot hear them, and yet she hears every word. Doctors have been of little help. The effectiveness of medicines has been short-lived. In her depression, she has wandered away from God. Despite all of the sleepless nights and continued torment, I am beginning to see this all as a gift—a gift that was given with a very specific purpose in mind. I do not yet know what that purpose is, but I am confident God will lead me in the direction toward fulfilling that purpose.

I prayed a prayer that I had prayed over my own house and wife: "Lord, I invite you into our home to be among us in everything that we do, to watch over us and protect us. Lord, I ask you to drive the demons back. Command them to leave our house. Post angels at every corner of the house. Post angels by every window, and keep the evil away from us."

My prayer continued for my sister. I asked the Lord that I may pray for my sister and call in the Lord to protect her and clear her house from this oppressive evil. I asked that I could pray since she cannot see past the darkness enough to pray for herself. "Lord, allow me to pray for her until she can find her way back to you and can pray for herself."

Immediately after my prayer, our pastor began to speak. He spoke of driving out the evil and demons that feed on us and drive us into depression. My mother, who is far more experienced in this than I am, said that was confirmation of my prayers. It was a message from God that I was on the right track.

As I am fairly new at this, I wonder to myself why God won't just come out and say, "Good job, Jeff, now you're getting it." I hear him clear enough about other things. Why not this? But of course, the other times I have heard him were at times when I was in great fear or when I had hit bottom. This was the time for me to learn, and to learn, I would need to learn to hear him in more subtle ways like through the confirmation of others. I took solace that God had let me know that I was going in the right direction.

That night, when Kelly and I said our nightly prayers, we prayed for Tina. We prayed a prayer similar to the one I said in church. That night, there was a new presence. It was very dark and hateful. I heard throughout that entire night that my sister was dead. They said she killed herself. Although I am beginning to see how frequently the enemy will use lies to get at me, this was a severe blow.

It was a very long night. The next day, I was filled with worry. I thought often of my sister then I thought of the confirmation I heard in church. Was this another confirmation? Was it a confirmation from the enemy? I didn't even know if the enemy could give such confirmations. This is my theory—I prayed, and the Lord confirmed my belief that there were demons tormenting my sister. When I prayed, the attacks from the enemy came quickly and unrelentingly. Every night I pray for my sister, the attacks come quickly. I think they recognize that my prayers are heard. They know how powerful those prayers are. They then become more desperate to stop my prayers, so they try everything they can to shake my confidence.

When they see that I will not show fear to them, they then resort to their backup plan: "Jeff, you are going to die! I am going to kill you!"

This again? "That will be hard for you to do from down the street. You are not allowed any closer."

"Do you really think so? Ha, ha, ha!"

"Yes, I do," I said. "The Lord protects this house. His is the only voice I obey. He is my Lord. He is my King. You are nothing to me."

A short time later, I heard an angry scream of frustration.

This went on for several days. On Thursday night, I heard them say that they loved me because I could hear them and I would not back down. This was certainly a new and unexpected tactic. Although it was a new direction for them, the point was still the same. It was a desperate attempt to get me to stop what I was doing, and what I was doing was learning about them. I was learning about the various tricks they use and how to resist them. I am an eager student. I will do whatever is necessary to learn all the Lord has to teach me.

Last night they said again, "Jeff, you are going to die tomorrow."

"Wait, didn't I die yesterday too?"

As much as I try to live a Christlike life, I cannot shake my attitude. My grandmother used to say I was being a wiseacre. When it comes to demons tormenting me and my family, I don't mind so much.

Friday, August 22, 2014

Last week, I received an email from a man I had not heard from in more than three years. In 2011, I had interviewed with a company based in Florida. Needless to say, I did not get that job. The president of that company is the one who sent me this email. They are interested in interviewing me for a different position.

So once again, Kelly and I are considering a potential move to Florida. With the unemployment of the past, I was eager to move. Now Kelly and I are growing closer to God and our church. I had such mixed feelings about a move to Florida. I did not want to stop learning what God was teaching me.

Later that night, sometime before bedtime, a thought popped into my head from out of nowhere: *To continue to grow, a plant must sometimes be moved to another location.*

This was no demon. This was not a quiet voice in the darkness. This was a thought delicately placed into my head as if it were my very own—except it wasn't my own. It was like the other times God had spoken to me, but it was different. This time it was not a voice and feeling that came from everywhere at the same time. It was as if I had the thought all on my own. The problem with that is that this was too philosophical and deep to be one of my thoughts. I believe this was the Holy Spirit telling me that a move would not stop the journey that Kelly and I are on. We will continue to grow and continue to walk the Lord's path. It has been something I have been praying about ever since I had received the email. It is not a promise of getting the job. It is simply telling me that location will not keep me from my path. It is a message that the Lord will follow me wherever I may go—even to Florida.

Sunday, November 2, 2014

This morning, Kelly went to church early for choir practice. I follow a bit later. When I arrive, I find Mom and Kelly. Mom mentions that Tina told her doctors when she was admitted to the hospital that she was worried about me because I told her I could hear voices. She was afraid of mental illness running in the family.

For a brief moment, I was saddened that she did not believe me. A thought then came to me that she is not supposed to believe—not yet. If she believed already, she would not see what the Lord can do.

I began to pray that the Lord would use me to show her that he is real and what I told her was the truth, and once again, a thought was carefully placed in my mind: *You believe, Jeffrey, but do you* believe? It was like it was a word for the church. I had never gotten one of those before. I was afraid of getting up and saying anything.

Just then, Pastor Steve gets up and gives a word for someone about fear. After Pastor Steve spoke, the choir began to sing the song from *The Prince of Egypt*. It was a song about believing and miracles.

Sunday, May 10, 2015

I was sitting in church this morning. I was praying that the Lord would fill me with the Holy Spirit. I was praying that the he would teach me to use the gifts he has given me. As I was praying, a woman in front of me sat down and bowed her head in prayer. I knew she had a few health problems. I felt pulled to place my hand on her back and pray for healing. I was reluctant. Why? I do not know. Again, it is the fear that makes me hesitate. Still, I felt the pull. It was a strong pull that I needed to pray for her, but again, I hesitated. As if responding to my reluctance, the Lord put the desire in the woman next to me to place a hand on the woman's back.

The Lord knows us better than we know ourselves. He understands our fears. He knows our weaknesses. He also knows how to give us a push when we need one. With that wall broken, I placed my hand upon her back and began to pray.

I started by praying the same thing I had been praying earlier—that I would be filled with the Holy Spirit—but this time, I prayed that the Spirit would fill the woman. After a short time, I began to pray to God about his healing miracles.

Lord, you have made the blind to see.

You have made the deaf to hear.

You have made the lame to walk.

You have made the dead to rise.

In Jesus's name, heal this woman.

As I continued to pray, the worship team began to sing the next song.

Our God

Water you turned into wine
Opened the eyes of the blind
There is no one like you
None like you.
Into the darkness you shine
Out of the ashes we rise
There is no one like you
None like You.
(Chris Tomlin)

It certainly sounded to me like it was a confirmation that I was on the right track.

A short time later, I was reading the weekly bulletin. In it was an advertisement for an upcoming seminar on activation of your spiritual gifts. Just then, a memory of a few months ago came to the forefront of my mind. It was of one of the first things I heard from the Lord: "You believe, Jeffrey, but do you *believe*?"

Only now did that statement make sense to me. It is easy to believe when the Lord uses someone else for his purposes. It is much more difficult to believe when it means the Lord uses you for his purposes. It has nothing to do with us doubting God. It has everything to do with us having confidence in ourselves. We have a tendency to find ourselves unworthy of what God would use us for. We can watch another person get healed, but if we are asked to do it ourselves, we suddenly have doubt that God would choose us to do it through.

I believed in the power of God. I believed that he could heal the sick. I doubted that he would find me worthy of such a gift.

A Light in the Darkness

Sunday, August 23, 2015

My world has just been turned upside down. More accurately, my world has just turned right side up. Never again will I view things the same. This was one of the greatest events in my life, making all of the torment and sleepless nights worth every moment.

A light in the darkness

There was a dream in a mazelike room. I hear a lion huffing—not a growl or anything like that, just enough to let me know he was there. I looked around the room I was in. I backed into a corner so I could see and not have anything come up behind me. It was a square room with a hall running along the wall to my left. It looked like a maze of some kind—not completely unlike an office full of cubicles except there was no way into the middle of the maze. The corridor ran all the way to the back left corner of the room. I glanced over the top of the maze as my gaze went toward the source of the sound.

A corridor matching the other ran along the right side of the room. At the back right corner stood a lion. It was a white cloudy mist that covered a what looked like a white lion standing in the corner. It had a translucence to it, but it was not enough for you to see through. The figure had a glow to it that shined like a light as it walked. I could see its white tail disappear behind the wall as it walked toward the corner at the opposite side of the room from where I was standing. I could still hear a light growl as it walked around the room. The sound grew fainter as it neared the back corner before growing louder again as it approached the corner to my left.

I saw it emerge from behind the wall and take a few steps toward me. It was just staring at me for a moment before taking a few steps closer to me. As it reached half the distance of the hall, it lunged directly toward me. It was a big lion that was nearly as tall as I am to the top of his head. It crouched down and leaped at me. There was no roar. I felt absolutely no fear. There was a calming and serene feeling as it hit me in the chest. There was no impact to the hit. It didn't really hit me as much as it went inside me. As soon as it did, I was burning hot—head to toe.

The intensity of the heat woke me from a deep sleep. I felt like I was on fire. I sat there for several minutes, trying to catch my breath and cool down. I quickly shed all of the blankets that were covering me. I sat there in bed, reflecting on the dream I had just had. It was so vivid. There was a feeling of peace and serenity surrounding the whole thing.

What happened next was most definitely not a dream.

It was only a few minutes later that a figure appeared next to my bed. He was tall with broad shoulders and a very muscular build. Just like the lion, he was a luminescent white figure that had a misty glow surrounding him. The figure was clear enough that I could distinguish the clothing he wore. I saw the features of his face but not well enough to provide much of a description.

He wore a uniform that looked to be some sort of armor. The helmet was a single round cap at the top that came down to the ears. There was a wrap that went from ear to ear across the back and down to the top of the shoulders, protecting the neck. I am no expert in armor, but I would say it was a lightweight armor of hardened leather—at least in appearance.

He stood at my bedside for perhaps twenty seconds or so. He scanned the room as he stood at his post. As he looked to the right, he momentarily looked down at me before resuming his scan. He then looked forward and began to walk toward the end of my bed and stood in between the bed and my wife's dresser. He stood there for a few seconds longer as he continued to scan the area. His gaze looked in all directions as he saw far beyond the walls that were only a few feet away. His appearance and demeanor reminded me of someone standing watch.

After surveying the area and apparently satisfied that all was secure, he took a cylindrical object, about three feet wide and ten inches around. It soon became clear to me that it was a bedroll that he carried. He turned the object on its side and unrolled the mat in front of the dresser. He took a few steps forward and eased himself down. At that moment, I saw another figure on the right side of the bed. This figure, dressed in the same fashion as the other, walked along my wife's side of the bed toward our bedroom door. As he approached the door, which was closed at the time, he did not slow his step at all. He just walked through the door as if he was going to check the rest of the house.

The heat was still present but not uncomfortably so. I sat there in bed, tempted to get up and check on the figure sleeping in front of the dresser. No sooner did the thought come to my mind than a heavy drowsiness overtook me. At a time when I would gladly stay awake to see what was next, I could not manage to even sit up any longer. I lay back on the bed as sleep took me as soon as my head touched the pillow.

It was a deep and dreamless sleep the likes I have not seen in many years. I heard no voices.

Tuesday, August 25, 2015

It was early in the morning when I awoke, around 5:30, I think. I lay in bed for a few minutes, letting the fog of sleep clear my mind and my eyes. Thoughts of the figures I saw during the night were on my mind as I sat up and got out of bed. I began to walk around the bed and toward the door when on the floor in front of our dresser, I could see what looked like a sleeping bag and pillow. It was not as bright as it was last night, and I could see that the image was beginning to fade. For now, it was still clear enough for me to recognize the wrinkled area where the figure slept. The sleeping bag extended the length of the dresser and about a foot beyond. It was real enough for me to walk around. I opened the bedroom door to walk down the hallway toward the kitchen when before me, I could see the figure from last night. He was walking about five feet in front of me as would a bodyguard. The image quickly faded.

I knew what they were. As sure as I have known anything before, I knew.

And this figure I now saw has been here for some time. Deep in the pit of my soul, I know he is the one who forced the demons from my home—an angel of God's own army, here in my house, watching over my wife and I. I had asked God for his protection. I had asked him to watch over my wife and I, to protect us from the enemy.

How humbling it is that God would send his angels here to my home.

I asked God to show me more. He has indeed.

Shadows

Things seem to be progressing at a fairly steady pace. What happened next should have been no surprise to me. For each step I take, I learn to control fear. I learn to trust in Christ. I gain an understanding of how the enemy works to try and push us off course. So why, then, every time we move to the next stage of my education, do I feel as though I have to start over? It would only make sense that what you have learned will be carried forward to the next lesson, right?

Nope. Well, not exactly. I carry what I have learned forward well enough. But as I move one step closer, the enemy ratchets up the intensity and hits me with something that I did not anticipate. In some cases, I do anticipate what is to come; but as I have learned, reality is far more interesting than anything we can imagine.

What Satan and his minions hit me with next, I could have predicted, but I could never have predicted the reality of how it felt. It began slowly.

At first the demons would tell me that the angels had left me. I could no longer see them, so they must have left. I was not worthy of the attention they had sought to give me and so they left and the voices continued. They were still some distance away and not screaming in my ear, but the persistence of their taunts began to take a toll.

It gets to a point that when I go to bed, I have to wrap myself up in the covers as if to hide myself from them. Continued calls of angels leaving me at their mercy were thrown at me. I desperately wanted the angels to return. I needed them to return. They were my protection from the demons. Where were they?

Sunday, September 13, 2015

The enemy will come at you from the place you fear the most, but what occurred to me was that it is not always about fear. Satan is very patient. He does not need to turn your world upside down to get at you. He only needs to rock the boat a little, and we will do the rest. In this case, it was not what I feared that he was to use. It was what I wanted the most that he used against me.

After I saw the angel standing watch over me, I wanted more. The third night I saw nothing. The fourth night, I saw an angel practicing his golf swing. I know, I know. I should have realized it then and there. Angels are ever vigilant and watchful. They are not there to practice their golf swing. But when you desire something so profoundly, you will believe almost anything.

The next night, I saw the shadows of demons. They were telling me that the angels were gone. They were telling me that I had no protection except them. For the next several days, I saw light shadows that the voices would say, "Did you see them? Did you see the angel?" Yes, I saw it, but was it an angel? Then I would see a shadow darker than the black of night.

"Did you see it? Did you see the demons?"

Yes, I saw them.

Would the angels really leave?

No, I don't think they would. In fact, I am sure they wouldn't.

This continued for several more days. I began to wonder why the angels that I was certain were still there—why would they allow the demons to taunt me? That is when it hit me. I was so foolish. God shows me his angels watching over me. Then the enemy shows me both angels and demons. They demonstrated to me that they could make the angels flee. What the enemy showed me were not angels. They knew that I wanted more of what God had given me, so they gave it to me. At least they made me believe they had. Then they made me believe that they were there as long as the demons would allow it. I knew that what they showed me was not the truth. I knew the angels—God's angels—had never left me, but that was not the point. I was filled with the Holy Spirit. That could never be taken from me. That could never be made to flee. Even if the angels were not there, the Holy Spirit was always there. I was never without the protection of the Christ. No evil spirit, demon, or Satan himself could take that away.

It is in times like these that I feel so foolish. God was teaching me things—that much I knew. For me to continue to learn, he must give the demons more leeway to work with. He must allow them to take the next step against me. This is a learning process. This does *not* mean that every time you cast out a demon, they return in a stronger form. This was how I had to learn.

I had to experience it and see it for myself. Every time I would wade out into deeper waters, I would have to fight my way through the fear and the enemy's attacks to find my way back to where God was waiting; and each time I would find my way back, God would smile at me with the proud look of a parent who watches their child walk for the first time.

And then he would toss me back out a little farther for me to do it again. The angels were still there. God was still there. The Holy Spirit was still with me. This was about God teaching me how to wear his armor.

And what I just realized is that for every increase in attacks by the enemy, God has given me something to strengthen my faith. First, it was his claiming Kelly as his own. It was a clear statement of ownership. Then it was hearing the demons being forced from my home. Then it was angels standing guard over my home and my family.

I have ultimate faith that God is watching over us and that we are working according to his plan. I will not let the foolish tricks of a demon shake that faith. I will learn what God has to teach me. I will learn to wear the armor of God—one piece at a time.

That was the last day I saw the false images that the enemy had been showing me.

Sunday, October 4, 2015

Another revelation. So far, in the battle with my demons, I have used music to block the endless barrages of taunts. I have been trying to sing only praise and worship songs to help me defend myself.

What I heard last night has led me to wonder if it is possible that the attacks go both ways. As I was singing praise and worship songs, the demons recite the words along with me in an effort to be annoying. They usually change a word here and there as to avoid saying anything compromising to a demon. For example, in the Lord's Prayer, we say, "Thy kingdom come, thy will be done." The demons recite the prayer but change the words to "Thy kingdom come, thy will not be done." This has become a challenge to me. I now try to sing songs in an effort to make them compromise themselves. I want them to sing that they are saved by the blood of Christ. This is much easier said than done.

But every now and again, they slip. As I was continuing to sing, the demon began to wail as in an uncomfortable pain, "Get out of my head!"

Monday, October 5, 2015

A new twist on the noises I have been hearing. For some time now, I have been hearing my phone ring at all hours of the night. I get up to check and see what is going on only to find that no calls have come in. I tried to silence my phone, but I keep hearing it ring. There were no comments from the enemy, so I did not, at first, make the connection.

They are trying to disrupt my sleep. Anything they can do to make me lose focus is tried. I shouldn't be surprised after all of this. Now that I have an idea of what is going on, that seemed to stop. Now here is the twist: Since I now understand what they are doing by making sounds of my phone ringing, they have changed tactics. Now I am hearing what sounds like a large window being broken. They follow this up with warnings of burglars breaking into our house.

Although I know what they are doing, the realistic sound of the glass breaking makes the whole ordeal very unnerving.

It takes me right back to burying my head in my pillows and singing praise and worship music.

Sunday, October 11, 2015

It's all about me

Kelly wanted to play hooky today from church. She has been like that several times over the past few weeks. This morning I almost didn't go. She was surprised that I did not try to make her feel guilty. I have done that in the past, I suppose. I have felt unworthy of what God has in store for me. How can I help anyone else if I can't help her?

Church began with me feeling discouraged. I was discouraged that I could do nothing to help her "reconnect" with God. One of the worship songs made me remember God's word to me many months ago when the enemy was threatening to take her from me and thanking me for giving her to them.

The words that I spoke were not mine.

"She's not mine to give," I said.

I remembered a year ago or so when she had her surgery. She was in the hospital, recovering. She told me she saw three figures watching her. I was not sure what to think at the time, but this morning at church, I understood what it was. Long before I had seen any angels myself, Kelly had seen them looking after her, and she never realized who or what they were.

She is not mine to give. She is not mine to protect. She is not mine to save. She is not mine to rescue. It is not my job to help her. The truth is it is not my job to help anyone. God chooses to use us. He will choose to use me—if that is his will—or he won't. It is entirely possible that this whole thing is for no other benefit than to bring me closer to God and to strengthen my faith. Somehow, though, I feel that there is more to my "education" than that. We are the instruments that he uses for his purpose. He has not protected her and watched over her in the past just to allow her to be led astray now.

Here I was, letting myself believe that it was *my* job to help her and make sure she does not wander off. Christ is the shepherd who looks after his flock, not me. If he wants to use me to give her encouragement or advice, he will give me the words to speak.

It's not all about me. It's not all about her. It's all about him. We only have to say yes when he calls us.

So when he calls, I, for one, will say yes.

Sunday, November 8, 2015

The hunter becomes the hunted

This week, a dramatic change took place. For so long, I have felt tormented by demons and evil spirits. My defense mechanism became singing worship songs to drown out the taunts. It has become second nature to sing worship songs to myself any time it was quiet.

This week the voices changed from taunting me to begging and pleading with me to "stop singing to the Lord of hosts." They begged me to stop. They could not take the worship music.

The hunter becomes the hunted. It was no longer my only defense. It was now a weapon to be yielded against the enemy.

My praise is a weapon.

I heard a voice this week. It was deep and gruff. I am not sure which it was, but it was a voice of pure evil. I continued to sing my praise and worship. As I sang, the voice began to lose its rough tone. It became smooth, and although still very deep, it was not as deep as it had before. It became the soft pleading spirit that begged me not to sing of praise.

My praise is a weapon.

Try to understand what an awesome gift this is. How can hearing the voices of demons possibly be a blessing?

My praise is a weapon, and I heard that praise slices through all of the taunts and attacks of the enemy as if it were a scene from a movie playing on a screen before me. Words have power, and I could see that power before me. Once again, I could see the power of the Holy Spirit. It was not just words or an idea that I could believe in.

Faith is believing what you cannot see. What do you call it when you can see and hear that power? It changes from faith to knowledge.

My praise is a weapon, and now I do not only believe it works—I know it works.

"I am not teaching you to hear them. I am teaching you to hear me."

Sunday, November 15, 2015

Praise and worship church this morning. This was the first song that was played—"Hosanna" by Hillsong United:

> Heal my heart and make it clean
> Open up my eyes to the things unseen
> How me how to love like you have loved me.

It continues to amaze me how so many songs resonate with exactly how things are going with me. They never hit home like this before, but as my eyes are opened to those "things unseen," they suddenly become more powerful than they were before.

Way cool.

Monday, February 22, 2016

It has been a good day. I got a raise.

I have been told that I can move to management if I continue to work hard and demonstrate my worth.

I should be happy. I should be thrilled.

But I just am. I have no excitement for what I do. I do it because it is a job, and it pays the bills. So I sit back and ask myself that elusive question—the question is not elusive, the answer is, and it really shouldn't be: If you could do anything for a living, what would it be?

Children have no problem answering that question. I am childish and juvenile, or so I have been told, so it should be easy. I want to be a firefighter, policeman, or jet pilot. That is what a child would normally answer. At least, in the old days, that is what they would have said.

Old days…

Does that mean I am old? I don't feel old. Well, not most of the time.

Sorry—squirrel!

What about me? What do I want to do when I grow up? I am not really sure. I know I want to have a purpose. I want my life to have meaning. I know, I know. All life has great importance and meaning.

Sometime in early May, 2016

The shadows that I have been seeing almost nightly have changed. The scene that unfolded before me was pretty scary even though I know better. I woke up and was staring at the wall that my side of the bed faces. A large shadow grows in the corner. I ignore and close my eyes to try and sleep. Not having much luck, I roll over in the direction of my wife. I see a shadow form a foot or two above her. It extended arms toward her. This was the first time that the shadow was anything other than a cloud.

Although my wife was sleeping on her stomach, it appeared as though her arms—or her spiritual arms—were reaching up toward the open arms of the demon. The spiritual arms of my wife were in a struggle with the arms of the demon. It was as if the demon was trying to grab her by the arms and she was struggling against it. There was a back and forth of pushing and pulling as the definition of the arms was lost in the movement of the struggle.

This demon was no longer a formless cloud. It was a…

I am not sure exactly how to describe it, to be honest. It had a head, neck, shoulders, and arms. I was going to say it was a human-oid kind of a shape, but that would be insulting to other humanoids as well as confusing things a bit. It was not in any way, shape, or form a human. The lower half from the chest down disappeared into a blur of inky black shadows.

I know this is just a demon trying to frighten me, but I wonder if there is more to it than that. Was this struggle symbolic of the struggle each of us face when our conscious mind is asleep? Do we all struggle with our own demons like this?

I have no answers to these questions at the moment. It is not like God gave me instructions to go along with each lesson I face other than the Bible, of course. As important and valuable as the Bible is, it does not explicitly cover many of the things that have been happening. Maybe this will become more clear as I learn. I will just have to put my trust in God and let him lead.

Friday, May 13, 2016

I had been tossing and turning for most of the night. Sometime in the early morning, I woke up rolled over to face the edge of the bed that faces the back wall of the house. There standing next to my bed was a tall figure. He was not as crystal clear as the first figure I saw, but he was there all the same. As I watched him, he walked up closer to the edge of the bed. He stretched out his arms above me as I lay there staring. His arms were about chest high and extended a few feet in front of him with slight bends to the elbows. He looked up for a few seconds and then lowered his hands. He took one step back before turning to his left and walking around toward my wife's side of the bed. He approached her side in about the same place and stretched his arms out above my sleeping wife. Again he raised his head for seconds before lowering his arms. It looked as though he was praying for us. The Bible does speak of angels praying and praising the Lord—not a lot of detail about it though.

He took one step back from the edge of the bed and turned to his right two steps forward and one to the right. He turned and took a seat at a chair (not one of mine, by the way) that was waiting for him. There he waited and watched.

A short time later, a deep voice in the darkness shouted, "That is not an angel! It is a demon. We are watching you."

A dark shadow began to form above my head near the bedroom wall that is on the side of the house. As the shadow grew, the figure seated near the bed jumped up and swung what appeared to be a sword toward the dark shadow.

The only way to describe the angels I have seen are like white figures. They are translucent but well defined. You can clearly recognize the sharp edges of clothing. They are much more than a "white shadow."

The dark figures, on the other hand, have no definition to them. They are just deep dark shadows that fill the area and grow in the night. Imagine something so dark that in the pitch-black dead of night, they still appear as shadows. They are not translucent. They create an empty void of black nothingness. That is what the demons look like that have been tormenting me for more than two years.

When the angel swung the sword, it was a narrow and shining blade that swung toward the darkness. The shadow retreated, but this back-and-forth dance continued for some time.

When you pray that God will watch over you and your family, this is how it happens: a guardian angel does not just sit by idly and watch. They are not there to give you a nudge when needed. They are not a heaven-sent GPS. They are there to protect you—and that is exactly what they do. They watch and observe. They command the evil to leave your house, and when necessary, they will draw their weapons and fight back the enemy that is so desperate to pull us away from our God. They cannot keep us from the eternal life that Christ sacrificed himself for—but a lot can happen between now and then.

July 9, 2016

I find that I have been a bit nervous when it comes to telling people about my book. I am not entirely sure why. I know that for every person that likes it, there will be ten more who think I am crazy and another four besides them who think I have a vivid imagination. I am not an attorney trying to convince people to believe in God. I think I am simply putting my experience out there. I will let people decide for themselves what to think about it. For some, it will be an awakening. It will open the doors to greater understanding of what may have been happening in their lives.

For others, it will be a lesson of how the enemy continues to try and wear us down. It may help them to recognize those attacks when they happen. Some will still be doubtful, but hopefully, it will open the door to a greater curiosity. While on vacation in New York, I told my sister-in-law about my book. She wants me to keep her posted. She was very interested. Perhaps this will be an avenue for people to ask some of the questions that they had been hesitant to ask before.

July 13, 2016

Last night, Kelly and I talked about people needing to see something to help them believe like seeing a loved one that has passed would help a person to have a greater faith in God. I asked her if it was like, "God, if you are real, show me something." I told her that was exactly what I said right before this whole thing started.

It can be difficult at times. I tell my wife everything. I keep no secrets especially in this, but I have some difficulty working up the nerve to tell her some things. I do not want her to be discouraged because I see things that she can't—at least not yet anyway. I do not want her to be fearful of some of the things I have seen and heard.

The last thing I would ever want to do is discourage someone during their walk with God. God has put me on this path. I have to put my faith and trust in him. I have to trust that he knows what is best and will not use this to make anything more difficult for anyone. I want to give people hope—a hope that God really is there and really does listen. Just because I can see and hear some of it does not mean that he is not doing the same thing for you right now. If you have prayed that God would send his angels to protect you, then he has.

Just don't be led astray by believing that God must not care because he is letting you go through some very difficult times, and don't blame it all on Satan. He is responsible for enough already without us giving him credit for other difficulties in our lives. Many of the things that we go through in life are necessary for building us up into the people God wants us to be. I wrote a poem once. Keep in mind that I am not a poet. I would scarcely consider myself a writer.

However, with that being said, this is the poem I wrote about a year ago:

> *Another piece upon the floor.*
> *Higher and higher 'til soon no more.*
> *Piece by piece my shattered life.*
> *I long to end the struggles and strife.*
> *I beg for help, but laughter hear.*
> *The shattered pieces replaced by fear.*
> *The smiling artist watches on.*
> *The only sound a mournful song.*
> *Is there no mercy to be found?*
> *My life builds up upon the ground.*
> *Is there no God to hear my plea?*
> *Grant me grace and set me free.*
> *With a smile full of paternal pride.*
> *The great artist by my side.*
> *There before us, a mirror be.*
> *And slowly I begin to see.*
> *Shame and guilt do fill my heart.*
> *Before me stands the work of art.*
> *Shaped in fire of holy grace.*
> *A tear I see, roll down his face.*

> *Listen to me, you who pursue righteousness and who seek the Lord: Look to the rock from which you were cut and the quarry from which you were hewn.* (Isaiah 51:1)

> *For we are God's handiwork, created in Christ Jesus to do good works. Which* God prepared in advance for us to do. (Ephesians 2:10)

You may not see it, but he is there. God has us in his arms. He has a purpose for us—if we are willing to step out of the boat and follow him. You may not see him, but he surely sees you. *He* has his hands out for you to grab hold of. What are you waiting for?

July 15, 2016

My alarm went off at 5:00 a.m. As is my usual custom, I snoozed for thirty minutes. I usually fall back asleep for a bit. This morning, I could not and just tossed and turned. Finally, I just lay back with my head against the pillow and stared at the ceiling.

I saw sparkles moving across the ceiling. Slowly they began to come into focus. They slowed to a speed I could see and moved closer. What I saw was the most remarkable thing I have ever seen— and that, my friends, is saying a lot.

The focus became clear as the movement stopped. It was a figure that I have become familiar with. When I first saw him, he was standing next to my bed, standing ever ready to do battle with the enemy on my behalf. There was another one above him that I have seen before as well. The most amazing thing about this new appearance was that they were flying.

Yep, you heard me correctly—flying angels! How cool is that!

Okay, I know what you are thinking. I asked the same thing. So let me get nerdy for a minute and give you my theory for how I could see them flying while lying in bed. First, the basics. When I first saw them, I was in bed. I saw them walking in front of me down the hall as well as walking around the room. Did I ever see them stop and open a door? Nope. They just walked right through them.

I think they are on a different plane of existence than we are. They do not need to use doors. The walls that separate them from the outside are as irrelevant as the doors. When they stood in my room and scanned the area while on patrol, they were seeing well beyond the boundaries of the walls.

The shadows that I see may, in fact, be looming above me from beyond my house. If God has allowed me to see them on their plane of existence, then I would conclude that I can see them beyond the physical limits of my home.

The one that I saw first almost a year ago was flying at about the height of the tops of the pine trees that are spread throughout my neighborhood. I would guess that he was a house or two over from mine. The other was flying at that height plus another half. As they were moving, their wings were spread out at their sides. There was some movement to the wings, but I could not describe it entirely as flapping. It was a kind of half flapping and half gliding. They did not need the wings to fly, as I could see it, but the wings helped the movement.

The one that was closest to me was scanning the area with his back facing me. He was in a standing position with his wings spread out at his shoulders. His wings were spread but were not flapping. He just appeared to be hovering as he kept watch. In one smooth and graceful motion, his wings swept forward, which propelled him backward and closer to my direction. As his wings swept forward, they tucked in closer to his side. As he moved backward, his left wing began to spread. With one wing slightly open, it caught the air, and he began to turn. As soon as he was facing in my direction, his other wing spread, and his turn halted.

It was a move that was so graceful it is difficult to put words to it. It had the gracefulness of a dancer. He looked down at me as I stared upward at him. His eyes did not stay focused on me for long. It was as if he was acknowledging that I was awake. He then continued his scanning of the area.

While this graceful aerial ballet was taking place, the second angel began to descend. Once he reached the altitude of the first angel, the white figure became a blur that headed toward my bedroom. It almost had the appearance of a beam of light. As it got closer to my room, the light faded. I could not see it in my room, but I knew that he had returned to watch over us.

The whole experience has left an indelible imprint on my soul of God's power and his love for us. Just the memory of it lifts my spirits in the days since. When I wake up, I can see the faint white glow as they fly overhead.

July 15, 2016

Demons can put images in my head—not sure how to explain it better. The thing about the images that makes things difficult is the fact that you cannot get away from it.

It is another lesson to never underestimate the power of a demon. Never take it for granted or become arrogant. Having great faith and confidence can lead to being arrogant. I have this problem from time to time. Sometimes the images are mild and just an irritant; other times, they are more difficult to put up with.

Occasionally, they get pretty bad. At least they appear to be heading in that direction. When they close in on getting worse, I see the whiteness of a shadow that is similar to the light of day shining through your eyelids. That light shadow sweeps the darkness away so I can get the sleep I need.

From time to time, I let my irritation and arrogance get the better of me.

Last night I saw an image of a demon drawing a picture as I lay in bed. This is not the first time. I immediately thought of a ten-year-old kid with a coloring book. *Great, a ten-year-old demon*, I thought to myself.

Immediate response: "*I am not!*"

Less than ten minutes later, the shower curtain in the master bathroom fell or was pulled down. This curtain has been in place for about a year. It is opened and closed at least twice a day and is fairly well secured. I know that it may come down if my wife or I slip in the shower and catch ourselves with the curtain. I could even understand it working its way loose, but none of those have happened. The shower was quite secure, and only minutes after I "insult" my demonic house guest, the shower gets yanked down quite forcefully.

Oh, and by the way, the shower curtain has the following Bible verses on it:

> *Believe*
> *If you have faith as a grain of mustard seed,*
> *you will say to this mountain, "Be moved from this*

place to that," and it will be moved; and nothing will be impossible to you. (Matthew 17:20)

Praise

Make a joyful noise to the Lord, all the earth; make a loud noise, and rejoice, and sing praise. (Psalm 98:4)

Serve

But as for me and my house, we will serve the Lord. (Joshua 24:15)

Trust

Trust in the Lord with all your heart; and lean not to your own understanding. (Proverbs 3:5)

Coincidence? I do not believe so.

July 23, 2016, last night to early in the morning

"Jeff, this is Santa Claus. You are getting coal for Christmas."
Umm, okay.
Usually I have something thoughtful to say about the taunts and torments I hear, but what can I possibly say to that? I am completely speechless—well, almost.
I have to be honest. I have to restrain myself from getting too cocky and arrogant. I have to watch my mouth because truth be told, I was tempted to return to the debate about the age of my tormentor. He claims to not act like a "ten-year-old," and he proceeds to tell me that I am getting coal for Christmas.
That is one piece of coal that will be proudly displayed on my mantle—if I had a mantle, that is.

July 24, 2016

This morning, my imagination was running wild as I was thinking of a possible future of what God has planned for me when a thought occurred to me. I was imagining myself casting demons out of someone's house. The demons told me that they are not afraid of me. I replied that of course, they are not afraid of me. I am only there to share the truth. The truth is what they fear.

The enemy fears the truth, and the truth will set us free.

That is rather profound, isn't it?

John F. Kennedy said, "There is nothing to fear but fear itself."

For us, fear is a weight that keeps us from trying new things. It prevents us from mending old fences. It prevents us from doing the right thing when we know we should. It is like being a bystander to a crime or injustice and not stepping forward. It is not just a weight; it is like a blanket that has been woven with concrete. If we act quickly enough when we first recognize the fear beginning to rise, we can push the blanket of fear aside and rise above it. The longer we wait, however, the concrete fibers of our blanket begin to harden. We struggle with the weight of it. It takes more effort to overcome. Often it requires the help of others to pull us out.

I have heard people talk about the fear of skydiving. They say that when the time comes to jump, they just do it. Any hesitation allows the fear to take hold. It can take an enormous amount of courage to overcome your fear or a seven-year-old girl.

When I was in the Marine Corps in the early nineties, I was stationed in Hawaii. It was fantastic. The nature that surrounds everything was a testament to God's handiwork. We would often go hiking in one of the many places nearby. We even went cliff diving once. Well, I went once. Others went more often. The cliff was about forty feet high. There was pool of deep-blue water at its base. It was an amazing sight to see. One after another, people walked toward the edge and jumped. Some took a little longer before they could build the nerve. I too took a little too long. I made the mistake of walking to the edge and looking down first—big mistake.

The fear slowly set in. I began to think how insane the idea of jumping was. That blanket of fear was beginning to set—and then it happened. Not even pausing for a moment, she ran to the edge and flung herself off the cliff, little blonde pigtails flowing in the breeze. She looked about seven. Talk about peer pressure. I would *never* live it down. A Marine who let a cliff in Hawaii and a seven-year-old get the best of him. So I jumped—and it was amazing.

Not quite so amazing as to try it again, but it was still pretty amazing.

Thanks to a little girl with pigtails.

Fear.

Don't hesitate.

Act.

Now.

The enemy knows how to play on our fear. That is what they do best—every fear, every insecurity.

Do you have a phobia? Spiders maybe? The enemy knows that. If given a chance, they will use it to their advantage, but you don't need me to tell you about our fears. We know what they are. We know how difficult they can be to overcome.

July 28, 2016

A man that I work with stopped by my office today in need of some computer help. I had been in a meeting for the first four hours of the day and had just returned to my office. Under normal circumstances, I would have a dozen voicemails and countless more emails to require my attention. For some reason, today I had neither. I am the resident IT person, and so he was hoping I could help him with a computer problem. A program he had been using gave him an error message saying there were not enough user licenses available and he could not access the program. To my knowledge, there is no such licensing for this program. He asked me, as he always does, how Kelly was doing. He is one of the kindest people I know. I, in turn, asked him how his son and girlfriend were doing.

We talked for a minute or two before he asked me how my book was coming. For the first time, I felt pulled to tell someone my story. As a Christian, he was very interested. He listened with rapt attention. I told him of how God was very real and how he answers prayers. I have seen those prayers get answered. He slowly began to tell me of something he had done wrong in his past. He told me of how it had been haunting him lately. He kept seeing the face of a person he had wronged many years ago everywhere he went. I do not know the details of this past sin. I do not need to know them. Christ paid for these sins. He paid a heavy price for them. He was betrayed, beaten beyond belief, and executed—everything done as the ultimate sacrifice to pay for our sins.

The big thing is he did not die for *all* of our sins. He died for *each* of our sins. There is a big difference. All would imply that he died for all of us at the same time—one life for billions—but that is not the case. He died for each of us, one by one.

I am not a counselor. I am not a therapist. But I *am* one who has seen darkness. I have seen the enemy work his way through his playbook of torments. He will take our weakness, however small, and cause it to grow beyond our control. It is very difficult to defend against these attacks of the enemy for the simple reason that you don't know you are being attacked in the first place. Defending against a threat that is both unseen and unheard is a monumental uphill battle. You cannot win this battle without the grace and love of God.

The only advantage I have is that God has blessed me with the ability to hear these attacks. Many of them I can see. This provides great insight, but seeing God defend me—that is where the real power comes in. Christ knows our weaknesses. He knows the burdens we carry. He also knows our hearts. He knows the regret and shame we carry, but now, he wants those burdens that he paid such a heavy price for. He is holding out his hands to take these burdens away from us.

And like so many of us, my friend has offered his burdens to Christ—offered, not give. We can hold out our hands to Christ for him to take our sins away from us, but we have to let go first. For some reason, we hold on to these sins as though our lives depend on them.

So I got up from my chair and walked over and closed the door to my office. I then turned back to my friend and sat next to him. I told him that Christ was waiting for him. He just had to let go, and he had to do it right now. We prayed for several minutes. I started, and he eventually asked God to take the sins that he has been carrying. We had been talking for just over a half an hour. He rose, feeling a bit better, and thanked me before heading back to his office.

I received a phone call a few minutes later. The problem he had been having with his computer was gone. It is all about God's timing. He knows our hearts. He has a plan. He will often put people in our paths for his purpose. We just have to be paying attention.

PART 3

Angels beside Me

The Battlefront

It has been some time since I have done any writing. I guess the problem I have been having is what do I write now that I have filled in the historical part. Truth be told, I am not sure. During my brief lapse in writing, I felt like I was letting people down. The point behind this book was to show people that the darkness that they are experiencing has a way out. I realize that a good 80 percent of the people who read this will think I am crazy. Then another 10 percent will be open to the idea of this all being true, but they will be a bit skeptical. An 8 percent will believe me completely.

That leaves 2 percent for all of you keeping score. It was for those last 2 percent that this whole book is being written. They are the ones who are living in a world of darkness. The depression and despair will be heavy. They will feel completely alone. Many will say that they understand as they too have suffered depression. Some may have suffered depression, but few will really understand what the last 2 percent are going through. I am writing the book, and not even I can imagine their pain.

The pain is personal. It is deep and dark. It is a life of solitude. Even in a crowded room full of friends and family, they still feel alone. No one can feel their pain—not really. Each is unique, but the feeling of being helpless and alone—that I understand. That is where there is common ground.

If you have stayed with me this far, you will know that I have been through some very dark places. The difference is that for a good portion of my time spent in the darkness, I knew I was not alone.

What God did with me was a bit different than most. At each phase of my journey, he gave me a tool to use before I stepped into the next chamber of this giant maze of darkness and fear. Most of the time, I didn't realize that he had given me anything to use—to say nothing about what that tool was. It was usually after I had used the tool a few times that I realized what was happening.

I thought I was losing my mind. I thought that I had finally gone off the deep end. Once you put your trust and faith in God, he will give you no more than what you can handle. That is very easy for someone to say until they try it for themselves. The truth is that God knew exactly how much I could handle. I, of course, had no idea. I felt like I was drowning, but to God, I was just getting my feet wet in the deep end.

If you can't swim and are tossed out of your boat, you will panic and flail your arms like there is no tomorrow. You see your life pass before your eyes. It is terrifying. Then God gives you a nudge and tells you to put your feet down and stand up. Only then do you realize you were terrified of drowning in three feet of water. It is impossible to understand until you actually stand up after going through it yourself.

You don't have to take my word for it—take God's:

> *This is my command—be strong and courageous! Do not be afraid or discouraged. For the Lord your God is with you wherever you go. (Joshua 1:9)*

I am not here to tell you that God will help you if you sincerely ask for it. He has already done that many times over.

What I am here to tell you is that God is real.

His angels are real.

That he hears your prayers is real.

That he answers your prayers is real.

And Satan? He too is real.

It is not likely that Satan is sitting next to you. He cannot be in all places at all times like God can, but what he does have is a nearly endless supply of demons to do his bidding. Those demons command still more demons and evil spirits—much like any other organizational hierarchy or army.

Satan sits at its front with several of his key demons. In the book of Revelations, Satan is described as a large red dragon (Revelation 12:3). At his sides are two other terrible demons—one who rose out of the sea and another who rose out of the earth in Revelation 13.

Before those two are countless other demons and before them many more. On and on, Satan's army is filled. In front of the many legions of demons are evil spirits.

That is one of the reasons never to become complacent or arrogant with the enemy we face. Every move up the ladder in Satan's army brings a bigger and scarier demon. I would guess that I have witnessed the bottom row of spirits and a few rows of demons. The ones I have dealt with are the low-level rank and file of his army.

Arrogance may move me up to a higher level of the ladder. And that, my friends, is not something anyone should ever wish for. Being tormented by demonic peons is quite enough for me.

That sounds pretty scary, doesn't it? It is.

But God's army is mightier still. Christ, the lamb, sits at its front. There are rows and rows and legions and legions of angels standing before him, and before them is an unseen army of warriors. These are the prayer warriors. They are people, like you and me, who dedicate their lives to praying for others.

This great battle is taking place right now. War as we know it is filled with the innocent civilians. Care is taken to keep them from harm. Sadly, mistakes happen. God's army takes great care in protecting those who have accepted Christ. Angels directly fight on their behalf.

The book of Revelation is about the end times, but that does not mean that they are all just staring across the space between heaven and hell as if it were a demilitarized zone like Korea. Battles and skirmishes take place all the time.

How does God win battles? By people giving their life to Christ. Once done, it cannot be undone. It is an irrevocable stamp of ownership. The course toward an eternity in heaven is guaranteed, but the path to get there does not have to be easy nor does it have to be straight. Giving your life to Christ can be a long and drawn-out battle all on its own.

Satan and his minions can't change the destination. All they can do is alter the route.

Remember that. It is very important.

It is also important to remember that Satan can win battles too. How does he do this?

By keeping people in the darkness. A person who is filled with sadness and depression is alone and in the dark. A person whose life is filled with anger and rage is alone in the dark.

He wins by keeping people as far away from Christ as possible. Satan's most powerful weapon is a lie. That is not to say that we are lying about the weapon itself. What it means is that lying is the most powerful weapon he can yield.

You might think that fear is the most powerful weapon he possesses. It is—at least in part. What makes fear so powerful?

Lies.

You are not worth anything.

You will never be loved.

You can't be an athlete. You are too short.

People are laughing at you.

God is not real.

He will not hear your cries.

There is no hope for you.

You are in the dark and all alone.

You get the point, don't you? These lies build fear. That fear is paralyzing. That fear is a debilitating master that can turn the strongest of people into hopelessly lost souls wandering through a giant maze of darkness and depression.

I was going to say slobbering puddles of mush but that sounds insensitive. I do not mean to belittle people who are suffering. You see, I too was once a slobbering puddle of mush.

So how in the mighty name of God do we give our lives to Christ in the face of all that?

That, my friends, is the greatest lie that Satan or any of his minions can possibly tell you.

You are in the dark and all alone.

How is that a lie?

How is it the greatest?

One would think that God's not real is the greatest lie. You can believe in God and still think that you are alone. If you are all alone and in the dark, what does anything else matter?

That is why it is the greatest lie, and that is why the lie is Satan's greatest weapon.

The Toolbox

Wouldn't it be great if God would just tell us what is going on or maybe just give us a quick tidbit to help us out? God will always give us the tools we need to get through difficult times. Maybe he could simply tell us what tool we will need so we can keep an eye out for it. We wouldn't want to miss it now, would we?

Let me have it, right? A tool to use on a difficult journey—like a rope to be used on a hike through the mountains, maybe even a life preserver if you are out in stormy seas. How about a paddle if you are ever up the creek?

That would be nice—or maybe not. The tools are seldom what we expect. Knowing what the tool is or the dangerous journey to be taken might be more of a burden. What if when Moses guided the Hebrews out of Egypt, God had told them that they would wander the desert for forty years and the only ones to see the Promised Land would be ones who had been born on the journey and never seen bondage? Would they have been as eager to flee Egypt knowing the hardships that lie ahead?

Who knows? That is impossible for us to tell. We can never presume to know how it felt to be in bondage for three hundred years. Even to die in the wilderness as a free people may have been better than to live in bondage. It is possible that nothing would have been any different.

But how about this—imagine we are Tom Hanks in *Cast Away*, but this time, God lets us know what lies ahead.

"Jeff, you are going to be on a plane, flying for business. It will crash over the ocean, and all aboard it would be lost except for you. You will be marooned on a deserted island for four years."

"Yes, Lord. It sounds like it will be the most difficult trial of my life. I will have faith and will persevere. What tools will you give me that I may survive?"

"Jeffrey, are you certain that you want to know?"

"Yes, Lord. I wouldn't want to miss it."

"Very well. To get you through this time of hardship and trial, I will give you a box that you may never open."

"A box, Lord. How is that to help me if I can't open it? Is there nothing else you can give me?"

"Okay, I have heard your pleas and will give you one more tool. Be careful with this one. It will be very important for you."

"Yes, of course, Lord. What is it?

"A volleyball."

"A volleyball?"

"Yes, a volleyball?

"I don't understand."

"You are not meant to—not yet anyway. In time, you will understand."

"Surely there must be more, Lord. There must be something else, right?"

"More? You want more? No. The box and the volley ball will be enough. No. I have told you too much already."

"But...a volleyball, Lord."

"And a box. Don't forget about the box? The box is the best part."

"Yes, Lord, the box. I will not forget about the box."

Gee, that would have made things better, wouldn't it? You would have taken the tools given to you by God and charged forward as if into battle—with your box and volley ball at your side.

Sure.

The point is that having more information will not always do what we think it will. What if you are told that you will get a flat tire on your way to work in the morning? What do you do with that knowledge? Do you change your route? Instead of taking the interstate, you take local roads. Maybe the local road is where you get your flat tire. Would you still have gotten the flat tire had you taken your normal route to work?

You may try many different things to avoid getting your flat tire, but what if while sitting at the side of the road, you meet someone who will change your life forever? There will always be something that we do not know. The sooner we come to grips with that, the easier it will be.

It is a matter of faith. God knows what he is doing. You can trust him to lead you through the difficult spots and give you the tools you need.

God has given us a vast array of tools and weapons to use in our fight against Satan and his army of followers. We only have to understand them and how they work.

So what is God's greatest weapon?

God's greatest weapon is also Satan's greatest fear.

So what is it?

Truth.

Oh, that sounds way too simple to be right. How can the truth be a weapon at all?

Truth is the foundation for the armor of God. It is a formidable weapon indeed, but it is the foundation of your defense.

The belt of truth

The first item we put on in the armor of God is the belt of truth.

As we are going into battle, we must first ensure that we are well defended. The armor of God is that defense.

The basis of that defense is the belt of truth.

Truth is critical to everything else that follows, but what does truth really mean for us?

Truth is built from four key principals. An easy way to remember it is the acronym SALT.

Principal 1: Strength

> But the Lord is faithful, and he will strengthen you and protect you from the evil one. (2 Thessalonians 3:3)

If you are new to the Bible, this might be new to you. This is God's promise to protect you and give you strength in your battle against the enemy.

Principal 2: Authority

> And these signs will accompany those who believe: In my name, they will drive out demons. (Mark 16:17)

Christ has given his believers the authority needed to cast out demons in his name.

Principal 3: Life

> For God so loved the world that he gave his one and only Son, that whoever believes in him shall not perish but have eternal life. (John 3:16)

This is probably one bible verse that most people have heard at one point or another. But what does it mean? Eternal life is pretty cut and dry. It does not say anything about having eternal life only if you can stay away from the clutches of Satan. It is unconditional. There is no power that Satan possesses that can change this fact.

Principal 4: Truth

> Then you will know the truth, and the truth shall set you free. (John 8:32)

Once we recognize the truth, we will be liberated from the grasps of the enemy.

So, how does this truth really set us free?

Lipstick-Wearing Demons

I was talking to my wife this morning about the people around us. Specifically, we were talking about the people that spew hateful and negative words to all around them. Their words spread like a poisonous cloud affecting all they encounter.

We all know people like these. They are all around us. For many Christians, this can be especially difficult to deal with. We spend our lives trying to follow in the footsteps of Christ. We try to set a good example for those around us. We try to have sympathy and compassion for the people around us.

But the venom that comes from their lips spreads like wildfire. People who have been listening to it longer than us have fallen prey to the poison. They have begun to allow it to continue without correction, or worse, they have joined in the venomous behavior.

How do we defend against that?

Kelly asked me why she had to hear this. It was like she had this gift to hear all the negative attitudes and poor behavior of people everywhere she went. It seems as though it follows her throughout her life.

Immediately, I thought of my own prayer to God and God's response that followed directly afterward. "God, why are you teaching me to hear demons?"

"Jeffrey, I am not teaching you to hear demons, I am teaching you to hear me."

The lesson is the same. The difference is her demons wear lipstick.

Now, before you get all judgmental on me, let me say this. In many cases, the demons we face every day are not demons at all. For these, we use the term *demons* quite figuratively. They are not the spawn and minions of Satan. More often than not, they are people.

January 23, 2017

I feel stuck. I am surprised at how long this has continued. I have continued to struggle with writing. I think of things to write at the most inconvenient times. Usually it is when I am in church or driving to or from work. It tends to happen when I am not near a computer to write things down. It is not like I am lacking in materials—the materials are here.

At church this week, one of our pastors told a story of a meeting he was in with many of his fellow pastors. They were convicted by the realization that God had become a topic to them instead of a part of them. I do not want God to be a topic of this book. I want God to inspire each and every word that gets written.

The verse of the day yesterday was Psalm 32:8–9:

> I will instruct you and teach you in the way you should go; I will counsel you with my loving eye on you. Do not be like the horse or the mule, which have no understanding but must be controlled by bit and bridle or they will not come to you.

This told me many things. First, God will teach me what I need to know. He will show me the direction I need to take. Second, he warns me not to be like a mule that is stubborn and will not move without much prodding. I must be open and ready to God's directions. All I need to say is "Yes, Lord."

Have faith, and the words will come. Be ready to say "Yes, Lord," and he will take the lead. There is a lesson in this for all of us.

If God wants you to walk along a specific path, will you stand steadfast in one spot until he tells you a direction? God will gladly give us direction. What he will not do, no matter how much we may plead with him to do so, is give us a swift kick in the hindquarters to get us moving. That part is entirely up to us.

Taking that first step is usually a tough one to take. Why does God not give us a shove? Because that first step requires us to put our trust in him. It takes a great deal of faith to step out even when we do not know the direction we are going. It is like Peter stepping out of the boat and onto the water in Matthew 14:29. It didn't take him long to sink, however, but he did take that first leap of faith. Stepping out in faith is not a single-step victory. It merely starts with one step. Then you give praise to the Lord for helping you to take that step. Then you take another step. He will be there to guide us and protect us. Ever vigilant the Father is over his children.

A child will jump without a thought of fear because they know that their parent is there to catch them. Why is it that a leap of that kind gets tougher the older we get? Because we can reason and rationalize things. Because we hesitate long enough with the door open and let fear creep in and overtake us—sort of like standing at the fridge with the door open, trying to decide what you want to eat for a snack with the exception that the container of lima beans is not going to jump out at you and petrify you with fear. I won't take any chances with the lima beans, just in case.

But how do you take that first step when simply getting out of bed is a monumental task? For those who are severely depressed, gathering that will is beyond comprehension. Go ahead and take that first step. That is easy for me to say, right?

I am not some all-knowing Christian with a hotline direct to God. I am just a flawed sinner who once begged God to show him that he was real. I am just a person who learned how to trust and rely upon God. I am someone who learned the truth.

You are loved. You are important. Imagine that you are sitting in your living room, watching the Super Bowl with a few friends. You sit and cheer for your favorite team. Things may have not been that cheerful in your life for quite some time, but I am sure that you can remember such an event. You can hear the cheers erupt as your favorite player makes a huge play.

You have such a cheering section. Imagine God sitting in front of a big screen TV with a few of his angels and saints. They share some popcorn and watch your life as it unfolds before them. Filled with drama and emotion, your story has their eyes glued to every moment. They see you about to take the first step in your personal leap of faith, and they begin to cheer, but you hesitate and do not take that leap. God may be all-knowing, but the angels sitting with him are not. They let out a sigh of empathy for you. Tears flow down their cheeks as they watch you.

"You were so close," they cry.

"Don't give up!" some shout.

But God, listening to their pleas, motions for them to settle down and keep quiet. "This is my favorite part," he says as he leans forward toward the edge of his seat.

All of the angels and saints lean forward as if it would help them to see it a little better.

Silence fills the room as your life continues to unfold across the screen.

But this time you, at your lowest point, give up trying to control what is uncontrollable. In a final act of broken surrender, you decide to take that step no matter where it may lead. You tried to do it on your own, and it didn't work. You are a little unsure, but you reach out with your foot as you take that small but crucial first step.

That is when you realize you have been holding your breath for the past several moments. As your foot moved forward and you feel the steady earth below it, you let out a deep breath.

From God's TV room, the crowd erupts with a cheer that would topple most earthbound stadiums. As proud as a father watching his child take their first step, God watches on. He knew you could do it.

But for you, in the here and now, preparing to take that step is pretty terrifying. My question to you is this: Why? Why is it terrifying?

Is it the thought of giving up control? Maybe that is it. Right now, you are in control.

How is that working out for you so far? Not so good, huh?

Realizing that you cannot do it alone is nothing to be ashamed of. It is a sign of maturity and growth.

> I can do all things through Christ who strengthens me. (Philippians 4:13)

You can do it.

I believe in you.

Christ believes in you.

Believe in him. Trust that he will take your hand. Trust that he will protect you as you walk.

We are not talking about a Neil Armstrong type of leap.

Just one small step—take it.

I promise it will change your life.

How do I begin to tell people of life-changing experiences? How do I begin to tell them of the battle that is going on around us? I sit here staring at my laptop, struggling to find the words that will do it justice. I try to think of how other authors would tell my story. Even that right there, "story," takes you away from the truth of it. The truth of it—think about that for a minute. Truth. That is what this is all about anyway. It is about the truth. Not my truth; I did not ask for this. Well, yes, I did. Everything that has happened to me over the past five years I asked for.

It is only by the grace and mercy of God that I am here to tell you about it.

The truth of the matter is also that it began long before five years ago, but it is not a story that I tell. Some of the definitions described by *Merriam-Webster* say that a story is a fictional narrative shorter than a novel. As with most dictionaries, there are multiple definitions listed. The first calls a story an account of incidents or events. Another calls it a widely circulated rumor. So the truthfulness of this story would be decided upon which definition you choose.

How about a testimony? A testimony is defined, again by *Merriam-Webster*, as "a firsthand authentication of fact." Another definition calls it "an open acknowledgement or a public profession of religious experience."

Testimony—that has a much more definitive connotation, doesn't it? When you hear the term "story," you have to judge whether or not the material you are hearing is the truth or fiction. But the term "testimony" makes you think of a statement made under oath in a courtroom. That gives you the impression that what you hear is factual.

As these events pertain to me, this is a testimony. I would declare it under oath before a judge in a courtroom. I would declare it before God himself on judgment day.

That sounds pretty confident, doesn't it?

About the Author

Jeff Daugherty grew up in a Christian house in Virginia, but like many people, he drifted away from God. After a divorce, three layoffs, and a bankruptcy, he began to question his beliefs and started exploring non-Christian beliefs in search of answers. Finding only darkness instead of answers, *Teetering on the Brink of Madness: Learning to Hear God* follows his journey out of the darkness and back to God.

Jeff studied theology at Regent University. He now lives in Vermont with his wife, Kelly, where he continues to write and study.